P9-DML-826

# FEEDING the BEAST

**An Insider's Guide to Local TV News**

## Tim Gordon and Monty Orrick

Cover Illustration: Gabriel Olson | Cartoons: Mark Plut

Feeding the Beast: A Handbook for Television News Reporters and Photographers

Copyright © 2012 by Tim Gordon and Monty Orrick

Cover Illustration: Gabriel Olson
Cartoons: Mark Plut
Editor: Monty Orrick
Cover layout and interior design by Masha Shubin

All rights reserved. No part of this book may be reproduced or transmitted in any form or by any means whatsoever, including photocopying, recording or by any information storage and retrieval system, without written permission from the publisher and/or author.

ISBN 978-1-4675-0284-9

Printed in the U.S.A.

1 3 5 7 9 10 8 6 4 2

# The Rundown

# Prologue

## Catching the Fire—An Adrenaline Rush

IT IS A QUIET NEWS DAY IN SPOKANE, UNTIL THE SCANNER STARTS BARKING. The noise is about a fire at a business, and they are calling in lots of equipment. Flames are visible and we are going.

Photographer Al Lozano and I load into a live truck, and get there as fast as we can. As we get close, the black smoke is an obvious column into the sky. Access is extremely good, just a half block from the burning building. Flames shoot from the cement block building. As Al sets up a live shot, I run to gather information. What kind of business is it? Is anyone hurt? They want a live shot as soon as possible to break into programming. This fire is huge, and suddenly even larger. As I run back to the truck, just on the other of the street, the roof collapses, and flames explode 150 feet into the air. I guard my face with my arm, the heat is intense. I can't believe how close I am, and the adrenaline I feel, experiencing this inferno first hand. I am focused, and smiling. Back at the truck, I pull a cable out for Al, he plugs in, and we go live. The anchor tosses to me, and I describe the scene. I am able to say that this is a motorcycle sales and service business. The fire started less than an hour ago. There are no reports of injuries, and there are dozens of firefighters on the scene trying to contain the blaze. But the pictures tell the story, and my job is easy and exciting. I work in concert with Al, as my words direct him to show what is happening.

"Look at these flames soaring into the air, on the ground here you see firefighters putting water on this building, oh there is another small explosion from inside the building". Classic show and tell, in the moment of breaking news, and we nail it.

After the live shot, we scramble to gather more dramatic images, get sound from officials and bystanders, find the business owner, and prepare for our early newscasts. The fire continues for a few hours, but eventually burns out the building.

My job as reporter is to help gather the elements, and then take what we have and what we know and create a meaningful story. This day we actually create several versions, one for each newscast. It is challenging and stressful, as I scramble and scribble. We are the lead and must make our slot. Then Al works his special bit of editing magic, just under deadline. We are drained physically and mentally, but sparked by the feeling that we have done our job completely and well.

## Did She Jump or Was She Pushed?

Kate Huether, a 24 years old woman from Portland, got lost in the mountains above a narrow twist of the Columbia River called the Bridge of the Gods. No one realized she was gone for forty eight hours. By the time her friends, landlord and parents could begin a search, with the help of local authorities and rescue volunteers, a small swarm of Nancy Drews and looky-loos descended on the trail head at North Bonneville in the shadow of that massive dam.

Completely innocuous, most people stop here for a potty break traveling east or west on Washington's highway 14. Other folks, like Kate, leave their cars and hike half a mile to roam the Pacific Crest Trail—an artery stretching from Canada to Mexico through some of the most sublime mountain scenery in the world. Today, however, the scene was not so lovely. That a girl was lost in the woods during a snowstorm was an optimistic scenario. One could only hope she had wandered off the trail. Of course, her family and loved ones accepted this possibility, but after two days of searching, every other person had their own theory—most half-baked.

"Why did the roommate refer to her in the past tense? He must have done something!"

"That trail side flasher snuck up on her and dragged her off the trail."

"She meant to kill herself out there. That's why she left her dog at home."

We forget that beguiling life and death situations are also someone's real-life bad dream.

Over the blacktop busy with people and vehicles came the unluckiest man, the lost girl's father. Apparently tired, he'd flown in from the East coast hoping to find his little girl rescued, but with every passing day a happy ending faded. On the second day of searching, he faced the phalanx of microphones and media to explain how he thought the search was going and describe his feelings.

Everyone knew this man was on the verge of the worst moment of his life. Losing a child. What could be worse? So the questions started, respectful but probing. Searching for something, Emotion without causing injury, if that's possible.

Eventually, the young woman was found at the edge of the woods below a two thousand foot cliff from which she'd fallen. She lay there almost a week and in view of the parking lot five miles away. With everyone wondering and looking and hoping, she might have seen us all down there if her eyes could have seen. The live trucks, lego-like from that distance with dishes upended. A temporary collection of people, horses and cars.

This rescue/recovery had a very large dose of what makes our job so interesting and different than most. Reporters and photographers get to be close to important stories where we live. Not inside the actual whirl of events, but near enough to feel it brush against us, so we might describe it for viewers and readers removed from the scene. This desire for a close-up view drives most photojournalists and reporters. We like to be where the action is.

## Written on the Wind

One of the odd features of this business is that our work is aired, viewed by thousands in the moment and then effectively disappears. Some stories have a slightly longer shelf life on a station's web site for a few days after the airing. There may be some pieces of stories that get re-used in promos. But the vast majority of TV news stories go out once over the air and are never seen again. They are Written on the Wind.

The print media has a much longer shelf life. Most stories from this decade are retrievable via the internet. Old newspaper stories are stored in libraries on microfiche. TV news stories from the last century are collected on film, tape (beta and ¾ inch) and hard drives and reside anonymously in dank basements or storage closets. Ninety nine percent of these stories haven't been seen since the day they were stored away. It's not unusual for entire tape libraries to be cleared out, making room for something the new news director considers more important. The collective effort by so many forgotten folks disappears for all time.

Maybe in a thousand years, a thirtieth century archaeologist will pull some old story tape off the shelf, fire up a dusty beta deck and see our world through the eyes of some ancient city's local TV news. They'll see what was important to us. What stories viewers liked. Events that mattered. What people intrigued us. These old stories would inform truthfully. Anguished or delighted faces, real sounds as they happened, the environment in and around our city. More than words in a print story. More than a dramatic movie re-telling. TV news stories will show who we are and how we lived.

That's what makes TV news great. It's real. That's why we love it and wanted to share it with you in this book.

# Introduction

THIS LITTLE TEXT BEGAN AS A QUESTION ONE MORNING, EN ROUTE TO A day's fishing. Where were the books that talked about local TV news from the inside? Why was every book on the subject a fancy, hardcover autobiography written by a famous anchor/reporter, or some dry textbook by an academic who hadn't worked inside a newsroom in years?

We thought then, as now, it is time for a personal narrative that brings readers into newsrooms, live shots and stories as they are breaking. We wanted to speak the entire truth on the subject. Ugly, cool and as much of the in-between as would fit.

The discussion of local TV news is dominated by a few groups. Business executives and the media corporations they work for will always have the final say. From office suites, they pull the strings that control what we do down in the field.

Academics and media watch dogs control another area of discourse. Usually, it's criticism—when we get out of line or our work gets sloppy or obvious. Occasionally, we are rewarded by the academics and institutions when they like what we do and give us awards.

Famous network anchors and reporters publish their autobiographies and life stories. Occasionally inspiring accounts about an individual succeeding against the odds, war stories and personal details that make them seem like the rest of us.

We felt there was room to inject a fresh stream of truth into the subject of local TV news. We wanted to turn an unblinking eye to it and attempt to describe this career objectively, thoroughly and critically—as we would approach any story assigned to us. Ours is an insider's look at local television news. Written by busy professionals, it was hatched one section at a time. During a hard day's work, some new section would present itself; the day's events would describe it. Our work-a-day world contributed to and informed almost every word.

We thought that to reach students and our colleagues, a book would be the best vehicle. We'd like journalism students to see what it takes to do this job and develop their own ideas about how they might succeed in it someday. For our colleagues working in the field, perhaps you'll read something to improve your story today.

We like the "Beast" metaphor to describe the news cycle and business we're in. Everyone in local TV news has used the term before. It fits, perhaps a little uncomfortably.

We are neither famous nor heavily credentialed academically. Tim Gordon, with a degree in Communications from Sonoma State University in California, has been a general assignment reporter doing local TV news for sixteen years now in five different markets (Billings, Montana, Lexington, Kentucky, Spokane, Washington, and Eugene and Portland, Oregon.) Monty Orrick graduated from the University of California at Berkeley, and has worked thirteen years as a TV news photojournalist in Eugene and Portland, Oregon. Before that he worked as an outdoor writer/photographer and documentary producer.

Our cartoonist, Mark Plut, has been a news photographer more than twenty years. That's a long time in this business. He's survived because he's got mad skills and a sense of humor about news.

In this book we're going to talk about certain things that do not change: telling good stories, how to make them good and what to avoid. We will also discuss some things that are changing very quickly: the new direction of local TV news and the new economics of big media corporations.

# A Greater Sum

The unique thing about TV news is that it is best gathered by two individuals. One concentrates on telling the story visually, while another considers what words to use in telling that story. The best word for it is "collaboration".

For this book, our voices are blended for most of it. But we wanted to speak to certain subjects separately. In order to do this, we placed an icon at the top of those sections where only one of us is speaking.

Tim Gordon's sections will begin with a notebook icon, like this one: ⬚ . Whenever the reader sees it, it's Tim's voice on the page.

To distinguish subjects concerned with photography, Monty Orrick uses this symbol: 📹 .

Reporters and photographers have a symbiotic relationship: different people with different tasks working closely together. Usually, we take something different from the same situation or subject. We thought the differences make this collaboration interesting and that we might learn something new by discussing our differences. We didn't hold back when we disagreed in order to throw the most light on this two-person job of news gathering.

We are interested in how our colleagues regard this book. Our goal was to give them something they could carry in their back pocket and refer to when they needed.

Running alongside this, was to keep our writing "in the moment" of producing local TV news. We wrote this way to include journalism students in the conversation. So they might get a fairly unvarnished look at our rapidly changing profession. An internship in a book.

# The Beast Master

## Our Shrinking Slice

THE DAYS OF EDWARD R. MURROW-STYLE JOURNALISM ARE LONG GONE, replaced by the brave new economic model of Television Journalism. Murrow set the standard, taking on subjects and people previously untouchable by mainstream media. The military industrial complex, popular politicians, unpopular wars were all fair game after Murrow. The tradition continued into the Sixties, with the Vietnam War and Watergate. Reporters like Safer, Wallace, Bradley, and others brought home the pain of the battlefield and national political corruption. With stories like these, TV news grew in popularity. Advertising dollars poured in and created huge profits for broadcasters. Local TV news became a cash cow for owners with a corner on the market. No other medium could deliver the news of the day in such an immediate, visual way. And the competition, just ABC, NBC and CBS, was a three team league.

The playing field has changed. Market shares have splintered to a fraction of what they once were, while viewers options for news continue to grow. Cable and Satellite providers offer a thousand channels with several score dedicated exclusively to news— national and regional. Then there is the internet. Information is available on demand with a click or slide of your fingertip. Why wait for the evening news? Go to the website and get it now. Of course, there is a deep pool of revenue there too, which broadcasters are dipping into as liberally as possible.

Another booby trap technology has created for TV news lies inside the tivo and DVR boxes which allow viewers to record, and then skip commercials. And yes, it effects local news programming, too. Just start watching the 6 o'clock news at 6:10, and condense your viewing time by skipping past the breaks. Advertisers desire rate cutbacks to reflect the trend.

So viewership and revenue is down. Yet many broadcasters expect the same profit margins for their product, including their local news product. They do this on the backs of the people who do the work: staff cutbacks, layoffs, reducing benefits and hours. Squeezing all they can from those that remain is the most common tactic. This creates frustration and discouragement for the people who must get newscasts on the air, from reporters and photographers, to producers and graphic artists. Some news directors may be adaptable enough to find a way to generate the anticipated profits while producing good local news. But they answer to the General Manager, who answers to the people holding the purse strings.

Increasingly, the money is controlled by large publicly traded corporations or worse, mega-private investment firms and capital investment groups whose main concern is profit margin. This is the Beast Master. A pride land hyena hiring businessmen to manage and demand thirty and forty percent annual returns on their investment. More people get laid off. Equipment failures aren't fixed. The current technology is replaced by automated systems. Under the guise of cost-effectiveness, streamlining and the recent HD transition, these systems force the elimination of many positions and people. Job snatchers. Those left to implement it know it renders a mediocre on-air product. The only time it's really spectacular is when it fails.

These seeming "improvements" are notorious for their lack of flexibility and the news product suffers. The threat of job loss hangs over anyone who disagrees with the new direction. Covering stories nobody cares about. Crime all the time, because it's easy. A water skiing squirrel "kicker" gave everyone at the desk a chuckle to end this vacuous newscast, while sensible viewers have changed the channel.

We take a more critical view of the current state of TV news because we live it every day. Some may walk blindly down their career path and do just what they are told with no debate. We say the best journalists should question, not only the story they cover that day, but also the business going on upstairs. If we don't fight back, the trend toward a cheaper news product will continue. If we can turn it around, TV news may again be valuable to the people we serve through the public airwaves. Fight the good fight, working within the system. Look for ways to make it better. Do the best work you can then we might win back some viewers and control over the stories we do.

## The Stories We Cover

The new economics of TV news has also caused a tidal shift in what we cover. Even while the revenue pool is receding, media corporations small to large typically realize profits of twenty, thirty and forty percent. Maintaining these margins affects how we cover the news in our city.

Carried out with the waves are longer format pieces, out-of-town, overnight and public service stories. Left stranded in the sand are the "quick turn" stories that are fast and easy to produce. Stories have to be turned in a day, and three versions, please. No more going out of town overnight to get deep into a story in some remote corner of the state. Except for the occasional investigative or sweeps piece, all stories get turned in a day.

The bottom line makes us bottom feeders. Some say that is the giant sucking sound that comes from local TV news. Crime and sleaze are easy. It takes less time to cover a shooting or methamphetamine bust than to do an in depth look at a bigger picture issue, like a social or economic issue. How quickly can you turn that story, and move on to the next? Given that kind of system, odds are it won't be an in-depth look at anything, no matter the subject. Odds are it won't be a masterpiece, either.

The new economics of news drives the process of determining what news is. The mill shutdown may affect a whole town and have larger implications for the state and even the national economy, but if it can't be turned for one of the early shows, it's not news. Not on television. It's a print story for the newspaper, even if it's visual, noisy and ideal for television.

What is news is the story you can turn in a day. Unfortunately, those stories get a little redundant. Car accidents, creepy neighbors, weather stories, gas prices and so on—all assume a greater news value because they're easy to do in a day. Are they more important than the mill shutdown? No. Are they more interesting than the mill shutdown? No. Do they have a greater effect on you or your neighbors than the mill shutdown? Probably not. But the fatal car accident can be reported in a day, give you a live presence at the top of a 5 and 5:30 and fill more time TODAY!

## News On Demand

Though the appetite for news is greater than ever, how we consume it has changed. We are no longer content to wait until five o'clock to turn on the TV and see the day's events. News consumers want to know what's happening when it's convenient for them. The desktop computer at work, laptop at home or i-phone on their hip, gives these consumers that option. They are not so interested in getting the entire story as knowing the most recent information. They may not even see the evening news when it airs. If they're interested, they may record it via a tivo-type device. But they will check out your website when they have time.

An analogy that describes this new viewer behavior is painting a house. Today's news consumers are perfectly content to watch the most recent stage of a house being painted. They aren't necessarily waiting to see the finished, painted home.

And so news outlets can no longer count on viewers coming to them at five o'clock. Rather, we must reach out to viewers and make our product available at their convenience. This obviously presents new challenges in satisfying these viewers. Getting pictures and updates on the internet as soon as possible is crucial. It is imperative those website consumers are steered to shows that evening where the entire day's details will be shared. Blogs are becoming more popular. These share a few details that are current even though they may wind up being a small part of the whole story. Similarly, a quick stand-up or a longer stand up called a "whip" might boil down a story in forty five seconds and go straight to the website. Even though a story may not be big enough to air live or break into programming, streaming it live on the web site is an excellent way to satisfy on-demand consumers.

This is exciting stuff. It is the direction local TV news is heading. The elephant in the room, obvious to crews in the field but rarely addressed by management, is how reporters and photographers will be able to produce the additional content necessary to feed the internet beast. While they tweet and blog away, they must also gather their story and produce several versions for the early shows.

Recently, in a station-wide meeting with a very senior corporate vice president, a reporter had the temerity to wonder aloud how they were to manage this work load. The executive's suggestion to save time and produce greater web site content, was that we should only do one interview per story. So much for balance or depth.

## The One Man Band

When reporters, photographers and truck operators are three separate human beings, the business of news-gathering and presenting stories "live" runs smoothly and safely. Perhaps as important as safety is quality in the stories we report and present live. Not coincidentally, it takes at least two people to present stories most effectively: a reporter and a photographer. Though any news person with experience in the field knows the advantage of having reporters, photographers and engineers working together to produce live news, nevertheless the trend is toward having two or even one person doing a story.

Anderson Cooper of CNN unintentionally threw a wrench into the spokes of two person news gathering when he shot a few of his own stories and they looked pretty good. That got everyone thinking about costs and management wondering why they should have photographers at all when reporters could shoot their own stuff. Most reporters prefer experienced photographers shoot stories with them. One station in San Francisco, the once respected NBC affiliate (now an independent), KRON has gone over to this type of "one man band" news gathering.

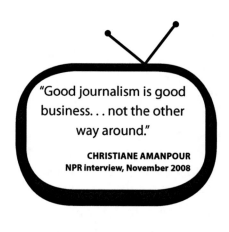

"Good journalism is good business. . . not the other way around."

**CHRISTIANE AMANPOUR**
**NPR interview, November 2008**

Their product is pretty shabby. And the station where Tim and I first worked together, though still deep-pocketed, has made the switch to journalism motivated by cost. Now, they scramble to keep up with a competitor we beat regularly just a few years ago.

It's not clear whether the one man band approach will fall from favor or not. But the entire industry is watching. This is the direction management would like to go though it's clear the scope and accuracy of individual stories suffers. If viewership declines too, greater cutbacks may be around the corner.

## Ratings

Measuring how many viewers actually watch any given TV show is called ratings. Nielson Media Research has a lock on this effort, and is paid by television station owners and networks to conduct the research. In markets 1 through 25 there are daily results, based on metering devices attached to televisions in a limited number of homes. In markets 26 and up, viewers fill out diaries, writing down what they watch during certain periods of time. These periods of time are called "ratings periods", or "sweeps". Ratings periods for TV are February, May, July, and November. July usually doesn't count much, as it's summer and viewership is off.

Even with daily meter results, the top 25 markets rely on sweeps periods and those diaries to determine what to charge for advertising time. The better the ratings, the more the station (or for nationally run spots, the networks) can charge for a commercial airing in that time period. This schedule determines how much revenue comes in, whether there's some profit and enough left over to finance a news operation. A simple equation that in many ways rules the work life of TV news people.

These are the times when newsrooms pull out all the stops to get people to watch. Efforts range from the well-told long form feature or investigative piece, to the over-promoted, salacious story about pole dancing or cell phone sex. Whatever we think will snare viewers. It can be good, and it can be ugly—more and more often, it's the latter.

You'll hear quite a bit about demographics or demos—not just how many are watching, but *who* is watching. Key demos are the people that have the money, and will spend it on what's being advertised. It varies—age 25-54, women, men, teens etc.

Soon "people meters" will replace the meters and diaries in markets 1-25, doing away with traditional sweeps periods. It's being touted as a more accurate way to measure viewership year-round. If we're lucky, this will lead to a practice of doing good stories that draw viewers all year long, as opposed to just trying to hook them any way we can every few months.

## Lead-Ins

Lead-ins are the shows that precede other shows in the broadcast day. Every show is a lead-in to what follows it.

News people care deeply about lead-ins to our newscasts. Do you have a good lead-in (meaning lots of viewers watching and sticking around for the news) or do you have a bad lead-in? Do you lose viewers despite a good lead-in? Do you build on your good lead-in? Do you build on a bad one? What type of story would tease or play well, considering the lead-in? These are all questions that get asked by managers, and that have some interest to the rest of us; especially in the top 25 metered markets where we can see our ratings daily.

Our little station pulled off a coup, winning the 11 p. m. news war in a May book. It was our first ratings win in a decade. Well, we are CBS. CBS has great prime time ratings right now, behind shows like CSI. So we had great lead-ins and we capitalized on them. The NBC affiliate used to be able to count on NBC prime time to give them lots of viewers. Remember Must See TV on Thursday? But NBC lost it, and the local affiliate has suffered for it.

On the other side of the coin, our local morning news ratings are abysmal, in part because of a long running problem with the CBS morning show, whose ratings are always in the tank. A lead-in is like a sharp sword that can cut you down or clear a path leading to success.

## Uncle Walter's Legacy

Two forces bang away at each other in local TV newsrooms every day. One is the insatiable need for content to satisfy the cravings of the modern news consumer. Not just video. Electronic content for the website is quickly catching up to video in importance and need.

"Just shoot a still with your cell phone, tweet a few sentences about the picture and send it to the web people."

Multi-media journalists are all the rage. Forget specialization. That's from a textbook long tossed aside. We need journalists who can do everything. Shoot the story. Voice the track. Edit the piece. Fire up the camera. Shoot the live shot. All by yourself.

You can do it. If you can't, step aside. We'll find someone younger and prettier who will attempt it for half your salary.

Orbiting in opposition to the new journalistic force of greater content contributed by fewer people is the binary star of ratings. To generate ratings, viewers must watch your news.

These two profit creating forces, low overhead and high ratings, are at odds. Fewer people producing more content equals a diminishment and dilution in your coverage that day. Is it really a good trade-off? Content for quality. A hand-written sign was momentarily taped up in an edit bay a few years ago before a manager removed it. It read:

*"Quantity is Job One."*

Those of us old enough to remember Walter Cronkite, even as children, knew instinctively we were listening to the most important stories of the day. These were condensed within the show for maximum potency of information.

Walter Cronkite worked from behind the same desk he sat at during his broadcasts. Hard copy wire stories piled up on it. Arguments about what should air or not flew across it. The best journalism of the day was concentrated above and around it. Just before the news was to begin, the paper, notes, cups and crumbs were swept from it and Walter Cronkite delivered The News from that desk. But that wasn't the last act. If important events happened during the 'cast, it was understood the newsroom's day included the half hour of the Evening News. It was all about the most important stories of the day, not the ones easiest to turn.

Spontaneity and live pictures are the norm now. Advances in technology come along so quickly, we barely have time to marvel at the progress before something faster and better replaces it. With all the satellite trucks and laptop editing, we can go live in a few minutes, but what have we gained if we have crank out four hurried versions of the same story and then write the web site copy? One step forward, two steps back.

Walter Cronkite never stooped to celebrity gossip. We appreciated the restraint in his personality, respected him for leaving his opinions out. When occasionally he let us know what he thought about a story, it was powerful. Now, idle chatter, celebrity dish and dumb jokes are the norm. It's no wonder so many educated people look elsewhere for information.

Why can't local TV news be the most authoritative voice for important stories of the day?

# Memorable Stories

## Story Is Paramount

Don't forget: stories have a beginning, middle and end. It's basic, but amazing how many reporters don't think about it. Set a high standard at the outset. Good story tellers set up the story with strong pictures (and hopefully some natural sound or short fore-shadowing sound bite) to create a sense of what's coming. Then the heart of the story: a strong middle with facts and emotion cul-minating in some sort of surprise. Then the resolution: an ending which is the strongest part of the piece.

The most important components of good story telling are (a) the facts, and (b) the emotion. Facts are the nuts and bolts: the who, what, when, where and how. Emotion drives the story.

Ask yourself a few questions What pictures and sound will best tell that story and evoke that emotional impact? Simple questions without complicated answers. Asking them early will get you on the right path and avoid wasting time interviewing people you won't need later.

Think about what your viewers want to see. What will satisfy them? Viewers want to hear people's stories, see and feel their emotion.

The greatest impact comes from focusing on a specific person within the group of players in the story. Avoid group interviews.

Finally, the best stories are simple. Complicated details dilute emotional impact. There is no room for pictures or sound that do not support the story. Photographers need to ask, does this shot make sense with the story we are telling? Is there another shot that will better fit the script. Reviewing their script, reporters should consider every section as to whether or not they can tell the story without this piece of sound or track?

The reporter needs to ask herself, "Are these the best words that tell the story and explain the pictures?" Be clear in your head whether you are advancing the story or writing to video because that's all most stories require. Waxing poetic without an accompanying visual component or moving forward the story is weak writing.

## Context

This word comes up often in reporter/photographer story discussions. The definition of context is "coherence". The TV news definition is putting something where it belongs because it makes sense. When we're out in the field we say we should include this shot or that sound bite because it "gives context" to the story we're telling. That means it helps the story make sense. It also may give clarity to a side issue that could confuse viewers.

## The Advantage of Context with Unavoidable Light or Sound Problems

Distracting sound or low light issues that cannot be avoided may work to your story's advantage if given context early in the piece. For example, doing a story about a micro-preemie baby sensitive to light made clear why the video was a little grainy (the "gain" pushed up a stop), and added to the story. Similarly, an over-active child whose exhortations might distract from interview sound can work to your advantage, if the child and their excitability are acknowledged early. Put in some natural sound of the kid then say something like, "this busy mom has her hands full." After that, any interruptions during her sound bites become a little part of the story.

## Seven Elements = A Story

One strategy for gathering a good story as quickly as possible is to apply the "rule of seven" as you drive to the scene. Whatever the story, consider what are three of the most important elements. If you gather good sound and compelling b-roll (pictures) of each of the three, you will then have six parts necessary to tell your news story. (Three different elements work better than two because they give roundness and completeness to a minute and half story.) The sound should be compelling for each element. That is, something emphatic and precise from the interview. The b-roll that goes with it should include sequences, some matching action, a little natural sound. Strong pictures tell the story at least as well as the sound bite.

The seventh element is a reporter stand-up. Shoot this in two parts by changing the angle and shot. Putting this two part stand up between the pictures and sound of three story elements will move your story nicely.

Late one December Saturday, my reporter and I were assigned to do a snowy weather story in Hood River, an hour away. We were also tasked with making the story about something other than merely weather. En route, we discussed the Seven Elements in the car and agreed on three: recreation, local economy, and transportation/roads. At the main marina, famous for world-class wind surfing, there were no wind surfers this snowy, freezing day. But there were two ladies walking their dogs and braving the wintry gorge wind. The dogs were frisky and one even "bonked" my lens in his enthusiasm. The ladies were not put off by the weather.

"Just because it's snowing, the dogs still need exercise."

We gathered our transportation element at the 76 station west of town. A lady moving from Hood River to Seattle that day and

13

a worker with a trailer full of heavy equipment bound for Yakima were both a little nervous about the condition of the roads. We shared what road and weather information we had. Hope they made it!

A toy store owner downtown was miffed that the arctic freeze was discouraging her customers and Christmas sales on this December 1st.

Any of these three little stories would have stood by itself had we more time.

We shot the stand-up in two parts. In the first part, the reporter stood at the marina and noted there were no windsurfers that day (shot wide with above a small bay empty of windsurfers.) For the second part, I placed the camera on the ground to match her observation that the snow wasn't yet sticking to the ground.

It was not as simple as it sounds gathering our story that day. The weather made it difficult to find people and uncomfortable to be out. When we finished our story about the snow storm in Hood River, it was well received and our effort commended. Both reactions are rare, so we knew we'd done something right. Some real emotion in the driver's fear. A laughable moment with the dogs in the snow. The Seven Elements approach kept us on that track.

## Where's the Juice?

Recently, we had a snow storm that made highway travel dangerous over the mountain passes. One road, in particular, had quite a few wrecks. Another just north of it had fewer driving mishaps, but was the main highway to the coast.

There was a lot of debate around the producer pod about where we should send crews that morning. One producer lobbied hard to send crews to the main highway even though the few wrecks there had been cleared. The logic went like this: viewers would be more interested in the road they usually take. Eventually, clearer heads prevailed and crews were sent to where the pictures and sound best told the story of the crazy drive to the coast that March morning.

News rooms, like reporters and photojournalists should ask and answer basic questions about big stories or breaking news events. What is the story? Where is the story happening? What are the best pictures and sound to tell the story?

## Meet Me Outside the Box

We pay a lot of lip-service to this cliché. You hear it batted around almost daily. In most morning meetings, an original story offered by a motivated reporter usually receives a collective yawn. This is particularly the case when producers are calling the shots about what stories are being covered that day. Original stories found by word of mouth or research are "enterprised". The print media recognize it as a very high form and give coveted awards for "enterprise reporting". Local TV newsrooms demonstrate a similar appreciation for stories viewers may watch only on their station by labeling it with an "Only On (fill in the number)" superimposition. And while fresh, original stories may find their way onto the airwaves, the herd mentality prevails. What's the competition doing? What's on the top half of the newspaper's front page ? What can we turn in a hurry? It's the lack of originality that makes local news generic and cause competing stations to air the same pictures simultaneously. These shows cry out for original stories.

## Help Viewers Understand Issues

In focus groups conducted by Crawford Johnson & Northcott in Fall 2008, viewers were more than ever angry, frustrated, even fearful about big news events. Politics, the economy, stories with disastrous outcomes contributed largely to the negative feelings viewer's felt. But it was the economy that was the root of the focus group's anger and most intense feelings.

This research is a giant shout out for local TV news to help ordinary viewers sort out economic problems large and small by giving them a voice. Local TV news can be a point man for clarifying and answering the larger problems viewers face. It's a good opportunity for us to inform, assist and in some cases defend people in our community. Done well, it might inspire viewers to look to the media for information during bad times and give us a chance to do responsible journalism that serves our city or region. CJ&N warned against becoming over-reliant on local experts whose answers might sound "pat". Stories should go beyond mere description of an economic event or trend. Give those affected a voice by doing interesting, informative stories for and about them. Find the answers they seek.

# Tim's Reporter Guidelines

## Laptop Envy

Despite the notebook and pencil icon to the side here, a reporter's tools are more technologically sophisticated these days. We are all moving into the 21$^{st}$ century, or if we are not, we are falling behind the competition. Next to his cell phone, Blackberry or i-phone, a laptop is a reporter's best friend. With wireless capabilities, information is always at your fingertips. You can research, communicate with the station or anyone else, and you can write scripts directly into your station's network and news software. It is a huge advantage in terms of producing quality work. We save valuable minutes that occasionally are the difference between missing and making slot. When stations fail to invest in this technology, they lose out. Every reporter should have a cell phone and a laptop. Better to have each reporter responsible for their laptop 24/7. Preferably, your newsroom desk has a docking bay for the laptop, so you simply plug in there when needed.

My current situation isn't that good. We have laptops in our three live trucks, but often they don't work. The operations manager believes it is because we abuse them. He is partly correct. We do abuse them. But only out of intense frustration when they "hibernate" two minutes before the script is due. Then they might have an unfriendly meeting with the dashboard. Yes, unreliable technology can be crippling, and send you back to a notepad in a hurry. You have to be able to trust and count on your gear. The best way to do that is to have one laptop, for you only, to cherish and use every day.

## Interview Technique

Being conversational is crucial to eliciting truthful, telling responses, the kind that sound good on TV. I generally try to strike a friendly tone in my interviews. You've got to ask the hardest question, but don't begin the interview that way. Diving in head first can be dangerous. Warm up to the tough stuff, if possible. Just like an ordinary conversation, you generally start with small talk appropriate to the interviewee. Save the tough investigative questions ("Why did your officer shoot instead of waiting for backup?") and emotional probes ("What will you miss most about Johnny?"), until you've developed a conversation. You'll get better responses from people who become more willing to open up.

For those anxious about being interviewed on camera, I often say, "Don't worry. We'll just have a conversation." It often helps.

Having a friendly conversation to warm up an interview subject isn't always the best approach. Sometimes you can sense a person does not want to hold back and needs to let it out right away. In that case, don't stop them. Also, due to time constraints you may only get a minute or two with the police chief—in that case, get right to the heart of it.

Before the interview, in the newsroom or in the car, gather some background about your story. If you have absolutely no knowledge of the subject matter, it's hard to know what to ask. When you end up asking "tell me about this" questions, you are not conducting an interview, but just taking what you get. With a computer and the internet at your fingertips, there is no excuse for not being at least a little informed when you arrive.

Take your limited knowledge and put it to work asking good

questions of people who are better informed than you are. It's one of the beauties of this job; you can learn something new every day. On the other hand, don't be a know-it-all. If you show up thinking you're an expert, you won't learn much.

Take notes as you interview. Sometimes it's a key word or phrase, to remind you of something. Or find its way into the script.

Don't lose contact with your interviewee. That means keeping eye contact, listening to what they say and having them look toward the camera. Profiles rarely offer as much emotion. Obviously when you do take notes it's okay to look down. Sometimes I'll explain this to the person I'm interviewing before we start. "Hey, I'll probably be taking some notes, so if I do, don't worry, I'm still listening".

Find your own style and methods that bring out the material you need for your story.

## Writing Styles—Keep It Active

Using natural, conversational language peppered with active and present tense verbs is the most effective writing style for television news. I have written television news stories for sixteen years. I believe I know what sounds good, and what doesn't. We've already talked about being conversational. That is the key to writing for voice, writing words easy to read aloud. Good news writing appears to effortlessly weave in sound from other sources: sound bites and natural sound.

Beyond that, write in the active voice. It makes a big difference in how a story moves and keeps viewer's attention. Active versus passive. An example of writing in the active voice: "The police apprehended the suspect", rather than "The suspect was apprehended by the police". There's much greater suggestion of action in the active verb "apprehended" than the passive verb phrase "was apprehended by". Look to infer action in your TV news writing wherever it fits.

Use verbs liberally. That makes for a sense of action in your story. Look for ways to describe actions that drive the story. Example: "Ben's mother <u>places</u> flowers at her son's grave. She <u>will never forget</u> the day she found out he had died". In this example I have also written in the present tense. This adds to the "activeness". The present tense is overused by some writers, which is annoying when the noun is dropped. For example: "Mothers find milk for the children, hoping their efforts pay off, building stronger bones." It's awkward sounding because nobody talks like that.

## Investigative Journalism

Investigative journalism is an often promoted but rarely practiced form of journalism in local TV news today. Sad but true. There used to be bigger budgets for real investigative journalism on local screens. That tap has run dry. Investigative journalism is time consuming and does not lend itself to turning out daily stories. The kind of developed skill it takes to really dig out the facts for such an investigative piece are generally not required to any great degree for general assignment reporting.

One local station in our market has an "I-team" (Investigative team) , but from what I can tell for the most part it's hype. It does however, offer a glimmer of hope. There is some effort there by a few reporters and photographers, my co-author included, to investigate issues that expose more than the average daily turn story. Most I've seen are consumer pieces, travel scams, bad landlords and dirty restaurants. That's better than nothing.

It is especially difficult to shed light on something others are trying to hide. But when you succeed, thereby helping the underdog and exposing the bad guys, it feels good. Sometimes it creates change in a broken system, sometimes not. But being thanked by an underdog for exposing wrongdoing done to them yields special satisfaction.

I recently experienced this with a story I did about overzealous drug enforcement cops who served a search warrant looking for drugs. When they didn't find any, they arrested the (drug free) parents on charges of felony mistreatment of their children for not having a clean house. Their home was messy, but not felonious. Though charges were dropped, the arrests cost one parent her job in the local school district, and hurt this family unfairly. It was wrong of the cops. We investigated and proved it. We gave this family their say, and offered the same to the stonewalling police department. In the end, the public response was strong enough to make the police think twice about trumping up charges, and also helped the parent land a new job.

If it's your interest, look for a place to work that has the attitude and resources to make investigative journalism a working reality, not just an empty promotional tease.

Good investigative stories expose more than one nefarious individual. Though that can be interesting too, if they're bad enough. But the important stories that win awards show problems in entire systems. Think Immigration and Naturalization Service, the CIA or a presidential administration. That's good stuff. Of course, a locksmith service that charges based on the value of client's automobiles is good, too. Catching anyone in a lie is good, but it's better if it's a big lie. Doing the research to uncover the details and paper trail of that lie takes time. Most good investigative stories take days to research and shoot.

My favorite stories catch people lying on camera. If that person is bad enough it's interesting, because it gets your hair up.

"How can they say that? That person is such a liar!"

If you can evoke that response in a viewer, you've got a good piece.

Whenever you can uncover something someone would rather remain unknown because they're scared or embarrassed or unsure, this may be the germ of a story worth investigating.

## News Bullies

This is a derogative term for investigative reporters and photojournalists who appear over-zealous in their reporting. Our experience is that reporters are extremely careful not to appear (on camera) to be bullying, badgering or inciting anyone. It looks bad. But there's a fine line between being the curmudgeon, asking hard questions, and bullying someone who doesn't deserve it. Usually we get called news bullies, or worse, by people who have been caught doing something they shouldn't. Individuals, officials and sometimes their attorneys, like to get in our face and make a big noise blaming us for what's happening to them. Increasingly, people scapegoat local TV news for launching them upriver without a paddle. It's a ploy used to confuse the issue and shift blame from themselves. Very occasionally, we do push people around more than we need to.

## An Eye for Details

Keep an eye out for details. This is true for facts, sound and video. As a reporter, cover the big, necessary facts. Then get those lesser known interesting tidbits to whip the mainline info into a richer, more captivating story. The same goes for video and sound. The obvious is easy. Adding the extras takes more time, but lends context, depth and flavor. How long your story can go is always a factor, but you'd be surprised how little time it takes to add a word, shot, or sound bite that makes the whole more interesting.

## Keep It Simple, Stupid

My first news director in Billings, Montana told me about the KISS rule in 1995, my first professional year in this business. KEEP IT SIMPLE STUPID! Though uncomplicated, the concept is sometimes difficult to accomplish.

You have very little time to tell the story. And if you're writing

a lot of flowery verse, you're not going to get very far before that time is up. You also probably are not writing to the video. Please be creative. Please tell me an interesting story. Please focus on the people you include in your story, and let them tell it as much as possible. But please keep it simple, stupid. This is not dumbing it down. It's about getting what's important into your story and making it understandable. It will make your life easier, too.

## Trust First Impressions and Ideas

First thoughts and inclinations can be good. Don't disregard them or let them drift away in the excitement. You can always change your mind, if you have time. Think about it. When you're conversing with someone, do you pick and choose your words cautiously, constantly rethinking and editing as you go? You don't, because you wouldn't get very far if you did.

After you know the video you're writing to, and you've considered the story's beginning, middle and end you can let it out, let it flow. . . Then go back and see if it works. If it doesn't, by all means change it. But don't discount your initial thoughts because you think you haven't tried hard enough. This goes for initial thoughts on interviews, lighting, camera work, etc. Once you are versed in the basics, make it easier on yourself and trust your first thoughts and inclinations.

One side note to keep you out of the boss's office: double check anything with legal/ethical considerations. If a red flag goes up in those areas, do not leave yourself unsure about possible legal or ethical problems that might pop up later. Ask someone who knows.

## Write to Your Video

Remember you *watch* TV. You don't just listen. The word television means sending pictures. So embrace the video, and write to it. Everybody knows reporters should write to their best pictures. Only a fraction do it well. When you log sound, take the extra five minutes required to log images. Then write to the best ones. Your final product will be instantly enhanced.

## Make it Fresh

One of the great challenges for writers in any field is keeping their work original. How many ways can you tell a story? The answer is infinite. But it's not always easy to come up with something new. We often don't have time. If we try too hard, we might just work our way into a convoluted, inferior script. Sometimes you must accept little victories, like starting or finishing a piece in some new way. Maybe it's how you string several sound bites together, or a surprise you're saving. Look for opportunities while being yourself. The KISS rule is a good start. Avoid clichés.

## Overcoming Writer's Block

If you're blocked, you're probably thinking or trying too hard. Don't hold back. Write down your very first thought about where to start.

Use chronological events to your advantage. Where does the story begin? Where does it go? Where does it end? Even if you're not stuck, it's a good place to jump off.

Sound often provides a good beginning. It may be the sound of sirens wailing, or debris crunching underfoot. Or a story setting sound bite.

"Why did he have to go so soon?"

Compelling sound can be motivation for a writer and a springboard for your thoughts. It is also an effective way to grab viewer's attention and get them into the story. Don't do it all the time, only when it fits. If it gets you going, it likely will get people interested.

There's an old axiom that your best video should roll first to grab the viewer's attention. Starting with it is another device for getting un-stuck. What video epitomizes or conveys the story best? What shot is so wonderful you must start with it? You'll find words that kick start the story, and give viewers a reason to watch.

Focus on one person and let the details of their experience move the story. It is a wonderful way to help you see the light through a fog of writer's block.

If you're not able to move forward, let your subjects do it for you, right out of the gate.

For example, if you have the natural sound of frogs on tape, start out with this. "JIMMY LIKES FROGS. THAT'S HOW HE GOT SO MANY OF THEM."

You get the idea. People are the story (and sometimes frogs are, too). Beginning with them will get you going, and carry you along.

Still stuck? Try writing or typing messy and fast. It's a stream of consciousness thing to let your ideas spill out. Fix it later. Don't break the flow by stopping and correcting spelling or punctuation errors. Keep it going, whether at a keyboard, pad or paper. I lose my train of thought stopping and starting. Then it makes it harder to finish. You don't have a lot of time. Make it legible for the person editing, but neatness doesn't count when writing for TV news.

 I think I agree with you, but I can't read anything you wrote.

## Talk to the Tie

 There will be the odd situation where a reporter may be an impediment to gathering a good interview; particularly when the subject is shy or disinclined to speak to the media. An example may tell it best.

The day labor site in Portland at the moment is not working too well. Many foreign-born day laborers prefer to find work off-site and avoid the hassles of signing up, taking a number and possibly exposing themselves to questions about their immigration status. We've encountered the worker's reticence to speak to the media every time we cover this story. The other day, my reporter, Bob Heye said: "I don't think these guys are going to talk to the tie."

He was referring to his work attire. And that these men, dressed for a day of manual labor, might be put off or intimidated by a guy in a suit. So I went out in less formal clothes, put the camera down on the ground and struck up a conversation. My Spanish ran out after a few salutations, but I got the main question across. Why don't these guys like to use the city sponsored day labor site to find work? They had strong opinions that were the crux of our story that day and necessary to telling it plainly. Initially, no one wanted to talk—even to a photographer dressed not unlike themselves. Eventually one did speak up and we got our interview, sound and story. But it took some strategy to get it. Reluctant interview subjects may talk to a photographer alone when they are intimidated by "the tie".

☐ The converse is true, too. Where the photographer needs to stay back until contact is made by the reporter. An example of this is when you are making a cold call at a home where the person is reluctant to speak on camera. The camera may scare them away. A persuasive reporter needs to make friendly contact first and work up to bringing a second person with a big camera into the relationship.

Every situation is different. Most of the time, you and the photographer will simply approach people together. No big deal. But be flexible. As a reporter or photographer, be ready to stand back and give people room to warm up to the idea of being in a TV news story.

## Writing Around Video

☐ There is a difference between writing <u>to</u> and writing <u>around</u> your pictures. For the latter, you write to the edges of your pictures. Here's the idea: instead of writing "Johnny spilled his milk" to cover that exact visual event, try to be a little metaphorical, or at least not so specific. Say "Johnny lost the last bit of nourishment in one fell swoop." Or more simply "One small move caused the trouble". This adds depth to the story. It's more fun writing to the edges than the exact center of the video, and more interesting because it's less obvious.

Think about how your words can support the video, not describe it literally. Choose descriptions that add depth to the pictures and give them context so they make sense and move the story forward.

## MOS = Man on the Street

☐ What does the "average person" think? This can be a useful perspective or an overused crutch, depending on the subject. It's easy enough to gather. Simply go where the people are, and ask them what they think. You will be ignored or told to go away, but there will also be plenty of friendly people willing to share their opinions. Some may be hard to stop! In any case, your best approach is to be warm and friendly. Turn on your natural charisma and you will be rewarded with the responses you need.

Don't confuse the news "MOS" with the film acronym, which stands for "mit out sound" (without sound.)

## See and Say

It goes back to kindergarten. What have you got to show me? Show and tell is a critical reporting technique in breaking news situations where little information is being provided. Just turn around, look at the situation, and describe what you see and hear, even what you feel or smell, if warranted. Work with the photographer to describe what pictures she is shooting, or direct her to what you want to talk about. The bedrock of good reporting is to be an observer at the scene.

## Networking

TV news is a personal profession, so networking with people who can affect your livelihood is important. They could be the ones helping you get your next job. Or bailing you out should you need it. I'm lousy at most of it: keeping in touch, making calls, e-mailing—kissing a little ass when and where required. It's a tough gig sometimes, but it helps to stay in touch. For co-workers you care about, remember they are the ones that count. Maintaining work relationships feels good, and could create your next career opportunity. As for the non-friends, be professional about it. Don't sell out, but don't burn bridges either. Sometimes co-workers you have the least in common with (often managers) can do the most for you.

I once worked for a news director that flew into town a few

weeks after I'd taken a new job there. She immediately changed my role at the station—the job I'd moved my family across the country to take. I did not like her or her management approach. Like a warning beacon for oncoming irrationality, her face turned red as a radish just before her not infrequent fits. She was hell for me and the entire newsroom. But I didn't freak on her. I smiled and found a new job with her recommendation. Not telling this person off, helped me move into a better deal.

I feel better knowing I have a clean record in terms of anger and vengeance. Don't burn bridges with co-workers you have trouble with. And keep regular contact with the ones you like.

## Developing Contacts

Journalism and TV news is a people business. Talking with

folks, from PIO's to people on the street, is an integral part of the job. You better be a talker, and more importantly a listener. Develop contacts, but beyond that develop relationships. They don't all have to be your friend, but they have to trust you and because of the trust, willing to work with you. Story ideas and information can come from police, junkies, court clerks, prostitutes and teachers. They will also come from your neighbors. If you have time, listen. And if it's worth it, keep listening. There are plenty of times I've had to cut off a druggie and move on with my life in order to make deadline. But there are other times listening for a while has been worth my time. Respect the folks you deal with every day, the cops and the clerks and the firefighters. Then they might respect, or at least tolerate you. And they will help you, if you develop that relationship and treat them fairly.

# Following a Story

Following a story that lives longer than a day is one the most satisfying aspects of reporting. In these cases, you can do much more reporting as the story develops. You get to know the people involved, understand their motivation. You dig for information, and report new developments as you get them. You can own the story. Following it takes dedication. If it was your story in the first place, don't let it be taken away. Dominating from the outset makes it difficult for managers to hand it off. Smart managers recognize the advantage of continuity in reporting an ongoing story, and want a good reporter to stick with it.

Keep good stories alive. What angle haven't you addressed? What new information can you discover? With whom have you not spoken that's deeply involved?

I've been working a story of an officer involved shooting that continues to unfold a week and a half after it started. I owned the story from the start by getting to the main players. Although officials aren't saying much while the investigation is ongoing, I am "in" with the family of a young man shot dead. Many circumstances of the case seem less cut and dry than similar stories I've covered. Why did the police use deadly force against a young man described as gentle and without any criminal record?

In the end, a grand jury decided the shooting was justified, but good reporting and asking questions of both sides kept my story in line and helped viewers understand the outcome.

Don't leave a news story that is ongoing. If you are at a scene and the story is changing, inform the desk of this dynamic situation. You never want to leave a story before there's some resolution. Otherwise, you might miss a dramatic outcome or miss reporting on how a story ended. Incomplete reporting is not appreciated.

## Checking Facts

It starts with the facts. If you don't get them right, the foundation is weak. The story that builds on those facts will not hold up. The first job of a journalist is to get the facts and confirm them. Facts make a story relevant and interesting. The big "nuts and bolts" facts are key, and so are smaller, more obscure ones.

If your first job is to get the facts straight, the second job is to use them in a way that creatively tells the story and engages the audience. I recently did a story about two guys who spent 17 years in prison on rape charges. New testing technology proved their DNA did not match any found on the evidence. As a result, both their convictions were overturned. Here's the first track I wrote for that story: "A handshake between two men who maintained their innocence all along—Larry Davis and Alan Northrup spent 17 years each in prison on rape convictions. Now free—and not going to trial again".

The first set of facts are there, written in a way that makes it conversational and interesting. Then I used a sound bite from one of the men: "It's been unreal, I mean overwhelming, great, awesome—everything else that goes with that", followed by another more detail-oriented track: "Wednesday, Davis and Northrup heard Judge Diane Woolard accept the prosecution's motion to dismiss the case against them. The Innocence Project used modern DNA testing not available in 1993 to free them. It proved that the men's DNA was not on the evidence. Davis was released from state prison in January after serving his full sentence. Northrup was released after a hearing in late March, when the judge overturned their original convictions. Now the state, after doing its own re-testing, agreed, the case should be dismissed." The sound bites and track use emotion to draw people in, and the facts to inform them.

Another aspect of your job is deciding which details to include and which to leave out. When there isn't much information in the first place, throw it all in. But too much information can be confusing. Decide what facts are key then balance those with details that best tell the story.

Don't believe anything you hear, and only half of what you see.

That attitude might sound cynical, but it's useful in the news business. You've got to have at least two corroborative, reliable sources for facts. Here's why.

Hillsboro around midnight. A brother and sister crossed a busy road. They had had a few drinks. They were jaywalking outside the cross walk. A city police cruiser plowed into both of them, nearly killing her. Big story for Sunday. When my reporter went snooping around MySpace for any information on the sister, her professional curiosity was satisfied. The girl's page had a name, photo and link to the brother whose address matched the accident location. We went right over and shot the accident scene as they were sweeping up. Later, we found the brother's condo a few blocks away, but no one was home.

When the story aired at five, what do you think we used for video and information? Because her name was not provided by the police or confirmed by any other source, we could not name either the sister or her brother. Neither could we show the brother's condo, which also fit the story. All we could use was some lame cop sound and the accident scene. We used the sister's picture later when her name was finally released by the police.

It doesn't matter how deep you get into an individual's personal information. If you don't have confirmation, you can't air that person's name, picture or information. Our dilemma that day was unusual, we had a lot of data that added up to conclusions that would have made an interesting news story. We were 99% certain we had our victim.

Even with information that makes sense, gut feeling and the possibility of breaking a big story, journalists who want to keep their jobs wait for reliable confirmation before airing names or pictures. Double confirmation is the best standard to keep.

Details and seeming facts get misreported every day. Naming an individual who turns out not to be involved is an unforgivable error in TV news that lands journalist's in that lonely chair opposite the news director every time. It happened a week ago to a reporter who named a child molester and showed him. Except it was the wrong guy. He shared a first and last name with the offender as well as similarities in ethnicity, age and gender. That's a lot to have in common and, some would say, an easy mistake to make. How many Michael Changs could there be living on San Rafael Street in Hillsboro? Apparently, two. This reporter needed to have seen a photograph (to possibly rule out the second man) or have corroboration from police.

At his desk, a reporter keeps a piece of paper that looks like it came from a fortune cookie taped below his computer monitor. It's the only thing stuck to the computer. It says:

"*Triple Check*".

## Three Questions

I know a local radio reporter who, every time we ride the elevator together at the police station, tells me the same secret to his successful career. He forgets he's told me six times already. All the photographers look alike in this town.

The last time he divulged his secret, it went like this:

"You know, I've made a career asking three questions. Who are you? Why are we here? And why is this important?"

Simple, right? This line of questions works and leads to other good questions and answers. Talking to strangers in elevators can be enlightening.

## Making the Call

Ringing the front door or phoning someone who has very recently lost a loved one is never fun. It's way up the list of Worst Aspects of the Job. But we have to make those calls and ring those door bells. Sometimes people will surprise you with their response, and if you handle it like a human being, it will happen more often than you'd expect. Be gentle, be kind, and if required, be persuasive in a fair way.

It's important to be persistent and consistent in your phone research. Call every number you have for a story and follow up every call that's returned. I was trying to get video of a meteor that caused a stir recently. It was impressive to everyone who saw it falling through the Earth's atmosphere. Five seconds of green, streaking ice ball. I called every institution that had cameras pointed anywhere. Airports, parking lots, hospitals, schools. Around the thirtieth number I dialed, it paid off. A hospital security camera above a parking lot captured the celestial event as it happened. It was the best video shot anywhere in the Northwest apparently and aired on news programs all over the world that week. If I'd been too busy for that thirty first call, no one would have seen it.

A Catholic priest in Newberg, Oregon drowned in the tidal waters off the Columbia River last winter. His brother and a friend drowned, too. Beloved by their family and fellow parishioners, it was a big loss for the church and town. That the deaths resulted from a boating accident made it news.

We went to the priest's church on Sunday, the day after it happened. We were turned away. The Catholic church and most churches operate like a corporation when the media becomes involved. We are usually not allowed on the property and get referred to public information people. Except being Sunday, we couldn't reach the church's spokesperson.

Standing off the property, the assembled media got a few shots from the curb. No photographs of the men were forthcoming and nobody wanted to talk. About this time, channel eight chose to leave. My reporter and I remained to get some sound.

Eventually, we spoke with two churchgoers who knew the men. When we went into the church after the service (without cameras) to inquire about a picture of the priest, we were turned away again.

When it came to the priest's family, whose address we knew, we elected not to knock on their door. We remembered this was likely the worst day of their family's collective life, so we elected not to intrude.

After we returned to the station, my reporter decided to call the family directly to ask about the possibility of getting a photograph of the men. To her surprise, the family was cordial and implied that we could have come out to the house after all—without imposing. We got the pictures and used them in our story. When Channel 8's story aired, we saw they had gone over to the house and interviewed the priest's daughter. She was relieved to tell them how great a man her father was. This interview happened shortly after they'd left the media throng outside the church. They'd made a phone call to the family.

## Do a One-Eighty

Don't let the excitement of breaking news distract you from

keeping your head about you. Turn your back to the event that has drawn the attention and take stock of what people are doing. There's a story on this side of the event, too. Who are the people there? Did they see the whole thing start? Are they affected? What's their story? Although some people just want to be left alone, it's amazing how many folks are willing, even eager to tell their story. It's okay to take advantage of a person's need to share. In some situations, people find it cathartic. Treat them with care and respect.

## More News Gathering Strategies

In breaking news situations crews must be prepared from the outset. It's good to have a microphone at the ready and switched on to get some sound. I conduct interviews as un-interview-like as possible. Keep it natural. This is easier said than done.

Microphone choice is the next question. The stick works best in fast-moving situations. Light and steadiness of interview (just bring the tripod) are secondary, but important to the finished package. When you have to work really fast, you and the person with the camera should strive to strike a balance between a naturally flowing interview and doing a perfect technical job.

When you're set, have a "high sign" between yourself and the photographer, a wink or whatever. It's much less intimidating for the subject than, "Are we rolling? Okay here we go". At times, you will be legally or ethically bound to inform the person that the interview is beginning, but rarely in breaking news.

For sit down interviews have the subject in their natural environment. If it's the mayor, have her behind her desk. If you want another look, have her perch near something that relates to the subject. If you're talking with a forklift driver, have him in the forklift seat. Keep people in their element.

Do not be late for press conferences. It's no fun to be the last crew in place, with a group either waiting or already started. Give yourself time to set up, put the microphone in a stand, position it, then arrange the lighting.

During the news conference, work together with the photographer, listen for good sound, and make note of time codes. When you think the time is right, get off the sticks and get a few different shots.

## Take Interview Subjects to Two Locations

I sat in on a Bob Dotson's NPPA Workshop Lecture in 2002. He recommended taking subjects to two different places and interviewing them in both. It took me a few tries before a reporter used sound from both spots in the same package. But the first time I saw it, I knew what Dotson was talking about. The story was better for it.

The impression is that you've taken time with the story, put thought into the subject and spent a lot of time with them. Two interview locations with the same person lends depth. The funny thing is that the impression is usually true. The story is deeper. You've spent more time interviewing your subject. You've probably thought about the questions a little more. You've given the person more time to think about their answers.

It's relatively easy and less time consuming than it seems. Just leave the lavaliere microphone on your subject after the first interview, then walk (drive, take an elevator) to a different spot. Shoot it differently, light it differently, different background. . . See what we're trying to do here? It may only take an extra ten or fifteen minutes. You may get a little walk and talk sound while you scout your second location. Of course, the script must contain sound from both locations. Reporters, don't be afraid to re-ask the best questions to elicit responses you liked from the first interview, so you've got good sound from both. The story will benefit from the little extra time you take.

Another interview situation also benefits from moving your subject to a different location. That is when the individual is not mustering any energy or enthusiasm. Some people freeze up and sound detached in front of a camera, even when they have seen something incredible. Even though the eyewitness is the person you want in your story, their sound may not be. In this case, just walk the subject closer to the scene they are talking about and ask them directly what they saw and where it occurred. This allows for a "brain reset". Most nervous people re-attach to the moment and act more like themselves when placed back in the scene.

## Balance

Wherever there's disagreement, you have the germ of an interesting story. Any story with two sides is best served hearing from each.

Time constraints may limit a reporter and photographer from being physically able to reach both sides before deadline. In that case, use the reporter track or script to express the other side.

There are stories that don't bother to balance two sides; where you hear from one person, what they think and why. These can be interesting and hold a viewer's interest. But, if you define news value as giving the best information so viewers can make up their own minds, the value of a one-sided story is less than a story with all sides. It is a reporter and photographer's obligation, as soon as they are assigned a story with two distinct views, to present both as roundly as possible.

Fairness is a more subjective goal that often rides in the back seat behind balance. News organizations like to tout their fairness, but it's more for public relations than as a real goal of news gathering. If a story is balanced, it should be fair.

## Reporter Presence

There is a place for reporter presence, as long as you don't take over and become the story. Sometimes the very best way to describe something is by showing it off. Demonstrating what

**Occasionally, reporters desire more shots of themselves than are necessary for the story. Editors call it "me-roll". Restrict shots of reporters to two types: 1) cutaways to avoid jump cuts like the shot above, or 2) genuine involvement with reporters asking questions or responding to the subject.**

something is or how it works may require your participation. A motivated stand-up moves the story forward, fills in a gap or provides a bridge to the next part of the piece.

Usually, you write up to a sound bite, but sometimes you've set it up best with the interview question. So occasionally, I leave my question or verbal prompt in a sound bite to add depth or context to a person's response. Don't overuse this, but don't be afraid to put yourself in there when it helps the story.

## Catch Phrases to Avoid

Call them clichés. They are descriptive phrases we've heard a hundred times or more, like "grisly discovery" or "unsolved mystery". It can also be a pairing of words that sound smart or professional, but lend little to the story like "all too" anything. Don't make me use it in a sentence, we're all too aware of this little phrase's inadequacies. One should avoid news writing that tends toward exaggeration. "Awesome" should not be used to describe any event other than a tornado, volcano eruption or airplanes colliding in mid-air. It's different if an anchor or reporter wants to describe something ad lib as "awesome", but not in a script. Slang may sound fine when you say it aloud in a script. We are supposed to write conversationally, but words like "groovy", "wicked" or any slang term don't have much descriptive traction outside of a narrow age group or era. News writers should be comfortable telling the story straightforwardly without pretentious language or clichés that attempt to cloak a story in an extra layer of importance.

We could re-title this section, Bad Writing. Here's a short list of some of the most egregious verbal offenders. Just to get you started. Each has its own particular stench; bloated, skimpy, infuriating or just bad writing. We'll leave some space at the end for whatever readers (and writers) might add. Remember, if it's healthy to love language, it's only natural to dislike some, too. Hate's a strong word. If someone says "don't be a hater", tell them you hate it when people say that. Here are a few phrases we love to hate.

**Due to**: Lazy writers begin sentences this way.

**Every parent's worst nightmare**: We've heard it a hundred times. It's lost its impact.

**It goes without saying**: Then why say it?

**All too**: See above for righteous indignation.

**Amazing story of survival:** Overused. Fine the first few times we heard it. But time to come up with something original.

**I can't believe it happened in this neighborhood.** But it always seems to. Avoid this overused soundbite, unless it really is a nice neighborhood, which it usually is not.

**Tragedy:** Dramatic, Shakespearean, overused. It's application, even correctly, makes earnest reporters sound shallow.

Suggesting we ought never use a cliché or well-known expression in a story is unrealistic. When you've only got forty five minutes to write a minute and a half package, you haven't time to re-invent the wheel. And some phrases (like, re-invent the wheel) get a message across directly. So, naturally, reporters will fall back on language they've used before for similar stories. Where does one draw the line? Dramatic stories require some drama in the telling. At the same time, one should avoid expressions we've heard a hundred times while simplifying language to fit the story we're telling today.

## Nine Eleven

Everyone remembers where they were and what they were doing. I was at home that day with my family. My oldest daughter, Grace, was just nine days old. I was in bed cuddling with my wife and baby when the phone rang. It was the station where I worked in Spokane, interrupting my family leave. A voice on the other end asked if I had my TV on yet? I said, "No. Why?" It was the executive producer at work.

"It's the end of the world as we know it".

It sounds a little over dramatic in the re-telling, but not at the time. She explained that a second plane had hit the Twin Towers, and there were reports of other hijacked planes crashing. She paused and went on.

"I'm sorry, but we really need you to come in."

I ran out to turn on the television, and it started to sink in. We were under some type of attack. With in-laws there, and a baby girl barely a week old, the tug of emotions started right away, and kept pulling. TV images sent a hollow feeling to the pit of my stomach. It was the Today Show, re-running that nightmare collision of aircraft and skyscraper. I realized along with everyone else that this was not an accident. Part of me wanted to cry, the other part wanted to build a wall around my house and family. As I showered and dressed for work, I wondered if another attack was occurring at that moment, wondered if we would be hit on the West coast, worried that some impending nuclear catastrophe might really cause the end of the world as we knew it. I thought about my daughter, and the world into which she'd been born. Could I keep her safe and secure in the years and decades to come? All sorts of grim pictures raced through my mind as I searched the closet for attire appropriate for this day. Then I had to try to put my feelings aside.

I covered the Red Cross first on 9/11. People were giving blood, trying to find some way to help. The blood would not be much needed, but the outpouring was a sign that people needed to feel useful in a time of crisis. The emotions people shared that day made for powerful television, but of course it came at an incalculable cost. I remember feeling a mixture of pride and sadness: proud of the people I met, sad for the reason of our meeting. That is often the case being a reporter. On this day, it was magnified.

As the day turned to night, I was moved to Spokane Airport and the nearby Air Force Base. Commercial air traffic was halted and I'll never forget the absolute quiet in normally busy airspace. The absence of jet engine sound and lights in the sky was ominous. Knowing this was the case at every domestic airport and airfield brought home the danger from above.

We ended up covering gas prices for our story that night. It sounds weird now, but on Nine Eleven people were concerned gas at the pump could be unaffordable, if world markets collapsed. Would people line up like survivalists to fill their tanks and spare cans? There was some immediate price gouging in parts of the United States. We found it not to be the case locally. As I recall, it wasn't much of a story.

Fortunately we were close to Fairchild Air Force Base, a major air-refueling base for the western United States. Enormous planes flew out of there to refuel fighter jets and others mid-flight.

Fascinating. I'd been on a refueling mission with them before—for a story. All commercial and private aviation was grounded that day, but military flight picked up by night's end. I am not an overly expressive patriot, nor am I particularly enthusiastic about military aviation, but when I heard the first of several KC-135 refueling planes take off, a lot of emotions came up. Next to my awakened love of country, I felt a commitment to telling the 9/11 story whatever way I could.

It was very good to get home to my family the evening of September 11th, 2001. Hugs were long and heartfelt. I counted all my blessings that night. That unforgettable day showed me how much I had and stood to lose.

## Eight Ideas for Story Telling

Consider "Hiker Rescue", "Icy Roads", "Body Found" or almost any story. These best way to pursue a story telling treatment is to begin by leaving the outcome in doubt. And find a person through whom you can inject that doubt. In the case of the lost hikers, find the spouse who's worried and get some pictures of that concern and sound to match. Begin with his worry. Show it. Since your opening shot cannot be of the rescue, start with a picture that sets it up: the spouse looking at an empty trail head or talking to officials then looking up the mountain. This way when the eventual rescue comes you've led your viewers down a path to that end. Don't give away your story in the first shot, track or sound bite. The story is, in a way, over at that point.

Whatever the story, tell it through a person. Elicit the main points of the story through your interview, so your subject may make the points for you. Tell as much as possible about this person as it may relate to your story then combine the facts, your subject/person and the little slice of their life you gather into a minute and a half package. Remember, this person and the story they are telling are all wrapped up in one story. Each may spill into the other. That's when you're rolling.

Present the story as a question. By leading up to the hook of any story by placing it in doubt or unlikely, writers give themselves the opportunity to create a moment when you finally reveal the fact. You've taken viewers down a little trail and shown them a view they weren't expecting.

Let the viewer realize something for themselves without saying it explicitly. Longer format pieces present the information without saying what one may conclude from it, necessarily. Just present the facts and story. Allow viewers to draw their own conclusions. But do it in an interesting, visual fashion.

Draw viewers in initially with a question or quandary which you may then set about answering in the course of the story.

Avoid the nuts and bolts re-telling. Force yourselves to tell the nuts and bolts with words and pictures outside the conventional.

Shoot stand-ups in, at least, two parts. No "walk and talks". Show something in the stand-up. Don't say something you could track and cover with video.

Hold out your best video. Have your opening shot be the shot that sets up the money shot, even if that shot won't appear for several sequences.

# Telling a Story with Pictures

## Getting Creative

You know you're in trouble when the reporter starts the day saying, "You're going to have to get a little creative today."

What this usually indicates is that the story has already occurred and you're getting to the scene late. No scene video, in other words. You, as photographer, are left with the task of telling the story as illustratively as you can without the actual event.

There are two solutions to this photojournalistic dilemma. Find an eye-witness or participant and tell the story through them. It doesn't hurt to overshoot this subject; you may find yourself telling the whole story through them. Have them take you to the scene with the lavaliere microphone ("the lav".) clipped to their collar. Follow them. Shoot them gesturing, speaking, walking into frame and out of it, listen for the good sound that often comes when people are walking around. Match action and sequence your shots wherever possible.

Another way to gather yesterday's news is to write the story first and get creative fitting pictures to the script. Enlist the reporter's help. They frequently have good ideas about pictures. A resourceful and imaginative news gathering team can create something from nothing. This is re-enactment, like the hour format shows "20/20" or "48 Hours" employ in their story telling. Sometimes an effect is thrown in for good measure (i. e. black and white, poster-ising or slow motion.) Viewers are sophisticated enough to know it's not the actual event.

Here's an example from last weekend: a story about a car chase and shoot out on a deserted road. Given the circumstances, an empty crime scene in the middle of nowhere with no eyewitnesses, it seemed our best bet was this second approach. If he wrote the script, I'd provide the pictures to move it. It went something like this.

"When the trooper got out of his patrol car, he got rammed, pinning him in the door."

This is when you have to get creative. I set the camera in the snow by the tire, began rolling then set my boot in the frame. Next shot, I cut to a wheel spinning in the ice as it moved out frame. Last and least effective, was a close-up of the car door not able to close because something was in the way. You get the idea, anyway. When the script described the trooper firing several shots at the vehicle, I shot another close-up of snow falling off a tree branch. It all worked well enough and under the circumstances, we were pleased with how the story looked and moved. Had the script not been written first, we would have been without these story telling shots. Most of these types of stories are reduced to steady shots of an empty crime scene with cop bites in between. Not very creative.

## A Basic Checklist

Some rules apply to every single TV news story whether you're preparing a piece for "60 Minutes", trying to make your slot in Spokane or preparing a class project. Here are a few.

**Listen to your interview sound through headphones** or your IFB as you record it to make sure it's loud enough and clean.

**Get an accurate white balance** before you hit the record button. If this is not possible, choose "preset" for the correct filter then white balance as soon as possible.

**Gather a variety of shots**. Wide of the scene, close-ups

of details that pertain, get near as possible to subjects. Shoot sequences of shots that match action when edited together. Allow moving subjects to go in and out of frame for snappier editing later. Use a tripod whenever you zoom in.

**Think about the story** and look for shots that tell all or part of that story.

**Punch the record button after the camera is steady. Record set shots for ten seconds**, at least.

**Follow movement until it's ended.** Then change shots or position.

**Make it original.** Don't try to do the story the way someone else did it. Use your professional acumen. Fall back on pictures you like best. If you see a way to tell a story using your favorite images, that may be an original approach to an old story.

## Common Mistakes

**Worst** are unmotivated pans, tilts, zooms and rack focuses. Zooms must reveal something important about the story. Whether you zoom in or out, some new detail should come into the frame that tells the story. Tilts and pans must be motivated by movement; either following the action or tilt/panning to an action. When your subject stops moving, camera movement should cease unless you're panning off the subject to show something in the near or foreground.

**Avoid** rack focusing on inanimate objects. A good rack focus ends on movement.

**Do not hesitate** to get off your sticks (tripod) and get into the action. If you're shooting off your shoulder keep it wide unless you've got some great action to follow.

In editing, build a bed of sound under your track and bites that pops up occasionally. Use natural sound to the story's advantage. Stories without natural sound are **flat and boring**.

**Not discussing the story** with your reporter doesn't help. Always ask, "What's our story? What pictures will tell it best?"

## Set, Sequential Shots Rule

I like set shots—moving shots must be motivated. I don't like flash for flash's sake. I'm old and don't ascribe to the Fox-ified way of doing things—maybe you do. In my book, well composed set shots in sequences rule. And please don't let the camera roll endlessly unless it's a riot or raging house fire. I only have so much time to log tape.

## Shoot and Move

Changing positions while shooting your story will benefit you in editing later on. If something repetitive is happening, shoot it wide, then move to a different spot and shoot the components medium and tight. Cut together for a matched action sequence, it looks better than if it were shot entirely from one spot.

H. Cartier-Bresson

**With still or moving pictures, the three most important visual considerations are subject, light, then composition. Combining them to tell a TV news story is what photojournalists do.**

When you see something essential to the story or very visual move to the middle of it. The most compelling picture is a wide shot right next to the action. The more you move and shoot, even hand held, the more options you'll have in editing.

It is best not to change your shot until the subject has stopped

48

moving or performing whatever they are doing. Changing shot or location in the middle of an action, usually leaves you with two shots that don't match or stand alone very well. A completed action cut to a different shot of whatever the subject does next matches and is visually easier to digest. If the subject is doing anything repetitive (photojournalists may look heavenward and point) than by all means change locations or focal length when you like. Matching everything up in editing creates continuous-looking action and stellar b-roll.

## Choice of Subject

Knowing what you are looking at through the lens is the most important consideration for a photographer. Whether you are shooting still or moving pictures, you have to think about the subject of every shot. What are you looking at when you're shooting? Is it in focus? If you're shooting an entire street scene, find a person or thing and compose the shot with them in mind. Be specific, not general about your subject. It translates to more interesting pictures and stories. Shots without a clear subject are not interesting.

The human eye is drawn to some elements in pictures and moving video more than others. First is an object that's moving and making noise. In the absence of movement, the eye will be drawn to the brightest object in the frame. After that, we look for color. The most attractive color to a roving eye is red.

## Shooting a Package in an Hour (or Less)

This happens a lot. It's part of the business of putting a show together every day. Ideas arrive late, stories fall through, producers get needy. Whatever the reason, the job inevitably falls to the photographer or, if she's lucky, the reporter <u>and</u> photographer to get it done. You're lucky to have a reporter for late assignments because they can tell you what they need as you go. Or what not to shoot. Don't forget to ask. You've only got an hour.

The first thing to keep in mind is: What's the story? Let's say it's a crime story that happened hours ago, but police just e-mailed a press release. You don't have a mug shot.

Arrive discreetly, and shoot aspects of the scene from the nearest place that allows some invisibility. Once you and your camera make the scene, people will leave. Bursting into crime scenes with cameras and station logos blazing scares away the people you want to talk to. Unfortunately, it also has the effect of attracting "looky-loos" and people who want to see themselves on TV. More than likely, other media are already there and keeping a low profile will be impossible.

Shoot any remaining police presence, tape, patrol cars, people milling around and any worried faces or reactions. Get sound from anyone who saw the incident or knows any of the main players. If you have to inform a bystander of anything to get a reaction, that's not as good. But with an hour to shoot, you'll have to get some sound, so it may be all you get.

Is someone watching from a balcony? Get a reaction shot first then ask if they saw the incident. Yes? Can they come down and talk? No? Can you come up? Yes? Bingo. There's your story, or at least a beginning and ending. Here are a few other ideas for good pictures and sound if you've only got an hour.

1. Look for details that tell the story. Close-ups of hands, shoes, faces. Tight as possible. Push the gain to get brighter through the telephoto. Anything moving is better.

Shoot any action or exchange as a sequence of shots. For example, a cop interviewing a witness. Create tension visually with a question. Who is the cop talking to? First show the cop asking a question to someone out of frame. The cop writes something down. Bystanders look on. Meanwhile, you're creating tension to be released when you show the interview subject. It's more compelling than a wider shot that shows everything. The four shot sequence lends pace and accelerates the story visually. You've got to do more with less. Show the wide shot eventually to set the entire scene, but only after the close-ups. It's not as interesting the other way around.

Shoot police lights as blurred foreground, in reflections or very tight. Be creative here.

When you're done and must leave to get back to the station, ask your reporter to drive around the scene while you shoot the scene wide from the passenger seat.

Editing run and gun stories must be done quickly. To save time, lay down all your sound first. A-rolling, it's called. Lay down the track, bite, track, nat sound, bite and so on. Once all the sound is edited, fill in the black holes with video. If Rambo were an editor, he'd work this way.

Run of the mill stories are rehearsals for big stories with lots of sound and pictures. Shooting a package in an hour can be a valuable exercise preparing you for the big story tomorrow. Coincidentally, these last minute crime scene or fire stories can also be fresh and exactly the story you've been honing your skills to tell.

If you've only got an hour, you'd better start talking before you get out of the garage. So what is the story? How do we get it done? Who do we need to talk with? With this deadline, every minute counts. Hopefully you've been given a head start by a crack assignment desk, but don't count on it. If you know where you are going, great—if not, figure it out and get there. And get to work. Some stories are easier to shoot in an hour than others. If all your interviews are at the location, it should be a cinch. If not, get ready to hustle, and BE EFFICIENT.

Pinning a lavaliere microphone on your subject is a good move when time is of the essence. You can gather an interview and then get natural sound of the person doing something. Some of the most interesting interviews happen while they sweep up the glass or paint over the graffiti. Black wires and wobbling transmitters are distracting. Hide them for style points.

Allow moving subjects to go in and out of frame. These shots fit anywhere in a story and make editing easier. Anytime you blend efficiency while gathering interesting content, you're performing at a high level.

## An Effective Mixture of Shots

The wide shot can be the most informative picture to convey a scene or place, particularly when the action is taking place three feet from the lens. A tight shot of the rock in the road where the slide happened and wiped out an automobile can also be the best story telling shot. Especially used directly before a wider shot of the entire slide and car. There's no hard or fast rule about it. That's what photographers get paid to do. Find the details, shots and sound that best convey the story. Then edit them together in the most interesting, informative way. A good mixture of wide, medium and tight shots is visually unpredictable and interesting. Wide shots should go after close-ups. Wide shots cut together without a close-up between them do not make an effective sequence.

There's an NPPA trick that sequences wide, medium and tight shots of one subject in that order. It draws you into the story. Move to change your angle at least once. It looks snappier when it's cut together.

I look for shots that are easy to digest and understand. A tight shot, simple to understand, is better than a wide shot with several elements that takes time to figure out. Give viewers an easy, identifiable subject of interest with other elements balancing it in the frame. The subject of a shot is whatever your eye is attracted to first. The subject can change to a different person or action and the camera should move to accommodate that. Any shot where the subject changes in the same shot is usually a pretty interesting, story telling shot.

**The near-drowning survivor works well as foreground. He gives three-dimensionality to the image and compelling context.**

Shoot from both high and low when the subject calls for it. Use a steady bag from the ground. Stand on a bench or roof of a live truck to get above the action and follow it around. Getting above the action with your tripod is even better because you can keep the zoom steady.

The appropriate camera height for the most interviews is chin level. Shoot the interview tight or wide, but keep the middle of the lens level with bottom of the chin to create tension. Think Hitchcock.

## Creating Tension or Why I Went to College

During my undergraduate years, my mother used to scold me. "If you spent as much time studying as you do in the record store, your grades would improve".

She was right. Except it was record stores, plural. Between my room off Telegraph Avenue and the Berkeley campus were exactly five record stores back in the day. Every day, I stopped at four of them. But I did learn a few things at the Big U. Some of them apply to my current profession. Miraculous! My mother would be so proud.

Film was my minor then and I took a class, Film 10 with Jonathan Rosenbaum. In it, we studied early Russian film-making. Sergei Eisenstein created conflict in <u>Battleship</u> <u>Potemkin</u> editing scenes into sequences where ships appear to be heading toward each other. In another scene, a baby carriage bounces down enormous stairs while peasants and soldiers run toward each other. All these forces in opposition render a feeling of conflict running under the action and dialogue. Though today's assignment on consumer credit problems is not the Russian Revolution, we can shoot and edit TV news with an eye toward creating tension when it fits the story. Tension is the news equivalent of filmic conflict and makes stories move more briskly. The film vocabulary for such ideas is richer than TV news, but in some cases, we are talking about the same thing. The Power of Juxtaposition.

Tension in news stories is usually created with sequences, like the cop interviewing a witness who's out of frame. Who's the cop talking to? What's he writing down? Now that you've created this little bit of tension/curiosity/conflict you owe the viewer some payoff. The last shot should be a two shot of the cop and witness or just a shot of the witness. This release is as important as the tension creating it. Tension without release is not satisfying and can be annoying. Look to create tension. But always with an eye and ear for its release.

Another device for releasing tension is leading up to a good sound bite. Cover the track that immediately precedes that sound bite with ever decreasing lengths of shot. Then the long, compelling sound bite releases the tension you created.

Showing interview subjects who disagree as talking heads framed on opposite sides creates tension, too.

Begin your package with a compelling sound bite or moment

that introduces the story by creating tension and curiosity in a viewer.

"Why did she have to die?"

"Who's to answer for this?"

"I don't know where he went."

Once you ask a question and create tension, you must answer the question in some way to release the tension. It's a pact between the story writers and viewers.

Tension creates curiosity. The film school equivalent is contained in the phrase, "suspension of disbelief". Can you get people to wonder along with you in a news story? If you can, then you're keeping things interesting.

## Film Language and Photojournalism

Ambitious news photographers look to films for inspiration and ideas, but it's important to remember the languages are different. Mind the gap. Film editing is about persuasion and influencing how a viewer feels about a character or story. The aim of editing TV news is objectivity and putting a viewer in the place and time of the story so they can make up their own mind.

## The Rule of Thirds

The most important photographic consideration after subject and light is composition. The rule of thirds is an aesthetic choice. It pleases the eye when used creatively. Virtually every shot, except the breaking news/following the action type of Moment, can be improved with a rule of thirds check. Whenever you frame a subject for an interview or compose a shot in a pleasing way, the "rule of thirds" has likely informed your decision.

Strictly, it is the frame divided into nine equal squares. The subject should be on one side, not square in the middle. The background belongs opposite the subject in the direction they're looking. Like every rule, this one can be broken when it improves the impact of a shot. Only after you understand *R3* completely should you break it. Otherwise, you're hoping for a happy accident.

You can get creative within the rule by applying it to up angles, close-ups, macro shots, <u>everything</u>. Any shot you see through a lens may be overlaid with a rule of thirds grid. As chess players visualize the board pieces to play matches in their head, photographers should look for the simple, beautiful rule of thirds in pictures, television, movies and everyday scenes. Know the rule well enough to use it unconsciously.

Ideally, your subject from one shot to the next will be near each other in the frame. Then you don't have to look around the new shot for its subject. Your eye lands there and there's no time lost trying to figure it out. This cinematographic concept can be applied to TV news and photojournalism, in general. Cinematographers from the 1940's were especially preoccupied with it. Watch <u>Citizen Kane</u>. From one shot to the next, your eye is already fixed to the general area within the frame where the subject is. Your eye doesn't wander to find what the cinematographer wants you to see. With every fresh edit, your eye is on the subject while your mind absorbs the scene, free to look around other areas of the frame for details of Charles Foster Kane's life. Again, today's climbing rescue story is not <u>Citizen Kane</u>. But when you're up there at Timberline Lodge at the rescue, keep your subject on the same side of the frame in matching shots. Then in a small, smart way <u>Citizen Kane</u> has informed your work.

## Crossing the Line

Whenever a subject directs his eyes in a specific direction (toward an interview, concert stage with audience, argument between two people), an imaginary line is created. This creates a problem in editing if you move around a lot. If you shoot the fire from one side then move to the other side of the line and show neighbors looking on, those people will appear to be looking the wrong direction when those two shots are edited together. If you don't physically cross the line, the subject and audience will always be looking in the right direction. Most photographers in this situation don't cross the line.

The visual construct is looser than it sounds. Any close up, macro or tight shot will smooth out a transition that has crossed over.

## Sequences

Nothing makes a news story move as well as sequences and matched action. It's cinematic and "two camera". Film editors call these match cuts. It gives a minute and a half news story a flow that straight shots can't catch up to. Look for action that can be strung together in several shots. My old Chief Photographer once referred to student protests as "a gift from God". Strung together carefully, the shouting, cut to the signs, feet walking, wide shot from the steps and back to the faces, can be a seamless sequence of as many shots. Really good photojournalists like Bill Goetz are always shooting sequences. That is, as soon as he gets a good shot he likes, he's looking for another one to match with it. You've got a grouping of crime scene markers near where detectives are standing. Shoot the markers and cop's boots. Look for a shot to match it. How about the cop's faces while they're talking? That matches action nicely and tells the story. Now, turn around for a reaction shot of nervous neighbors pointing. Back to the scene: shoot the detective laying down another marker by a spent shell casing. Edited together in that order, you have a sequence. The last shot, the detective laying down the marker, was probably shot earlier than the rest, but shuffled behind them makes for effective story telling without misinforming.

Shots in a sequence give a continuous impression of an event which mimics the way our own eyes and ears might perceive it.

Placing the camera in unusual places to get a worm, bird or salmon's eye view is good use of perspective and a sign of accomplished photojournalism.

## Perspective

Photographers can manipulate where they place their camera to show unusual perspectives and help tell the story. If heat has something to do with the story, set the camera on the ground or steady bag to get a telephoto shot of the subject with heat waves coming up from the ground, distorting the picture. You would never put your face on hot pavement to see this image, but the camera can do it and give you an interesting perspective.

## Proper Color Balance

What distinguishes good classroom projects from inferior ones is also what separates small market photographers from their big market colleagues. Accurate color balance and clean audio. We alluded to it in the section about fundamentals. But there's more to it.

Have you ever seen a movie with unintentional bad color or inaudible sound? Not really. It's not uncommon on public access channels and it's just bad. If the color's wrong it's distracting. Save weird color balances for art class. Don't bother with bad audio.

Balance color as near to natural as you can. Obtain your white balance by having your subject hold a white piece of paper under their chin. If you're using lights, turn everything on then balance for white. It's the last thing you do before hitting the record button, and the most important adjustment.

Photojournalists need to know how to color balance correctly. Two sections in the lighting chapter (Night Video and Natural Light) cover almost all lighting situations.

## Clean Audio

In a TV news story you must always be able to understand what you're hearing. You should never have to strain to pick up the words. When interviews or voice tracks are difficult to hear they were either poorly recorded or laid down too low in editing. The latter is a human error that is easily fixed. Recording sound at appropriate levels for editing and playback is a larger consideration. Record your audio loud, but don't overdrive it. In most cameras you can see audio levels inside the eyepiece. That's progress! Make sure the levels bubble under and seldom over the yellow line. That's plenty loud and distortion will be minimal.

The alternative is audio that's too low. This requires boosting which increases distortion. Every camera type displays audio levels differently. You need to know where the level is when sounds starts to distort from being too loud. Then back off a little. If you're audio is still too hot or low, run a test to find the sweet spot: loud, but not too loud. Set wireless microphones to transmit equally loud. Then you won't have to change audio levels on the camera as often.

In editing, set all your a-roll sound to the same level. Most non-linear programs should peak between -12 and -6. Once it's consistent, give it a listen for **apparent sound**. An ear check. Listen without watching the meters. Too loud or quiet audio may still be present and need adjusting. Slightly over-modulated words or phrases can be brought down with a few mouse clicks. Bring up sound bites that trail off at the end.

## Keep Rolling in a Riot

On the action, that is. You don't want to miss anything when it's hot and heavy. Just roll on all of what you see happening. Don't worry about burning tape or card space. The only mistake you can make in these rare, exciting situations is missing something important. This is true for a riot, a big explosive fire, or anything that is taking off at the moment you are getting your shots. When it calms down, you can back off, compose some shots, and fill in with what you may have missed in the frenzy. Reporters should watch the photog's back, run for that fresh battery or tape, and pay attention to your surroundings. Protect and assist your camera buddy to get the shots safely and without getting run over. At the same time, take quick written notes of what you see around you. Survey the scene for the best folks to talk to about the situation. If time allows, get some sound as the event is unfolding behind or around them. Stay sharp and be careful.

## Beauty Shots

This term is kind of a put down. Usually, someone in a news room will specifically ask for a beauty shot when they need video to run behind a weather graphic. They want an image thoughtfully composed with an element of still photography. Be it composition, light, a moment or all three in one shot, beauty shots improve the look of any newscast or story. No one ever said a shot was too pretty.

## Shooting Pool

This is not the game with pool cues and eight balls, but rather the responsibility of gathering pictures and sound from one event for all interested TV stations. We're talking crowded court-rooms, funerals and interviews with subjects who want to limit media access. In these circumstances, one photographer is selected to shoot for all. The usual protocol is that anyone who wants a dub (copy) of the tape must be present at the event while it's occurring. Don't show up after the trial and expect a dub.

There's an added level of responsibility to being the "pool cam". All the media outlets receiving copies of your work will be limited to what you shoot. Attempt to gather enough elements, even from a quick arraignment, to make an entire package. If this seems like too much effort for a two minute arraignment, imagine the other photographer who has to edit a minute and a half package

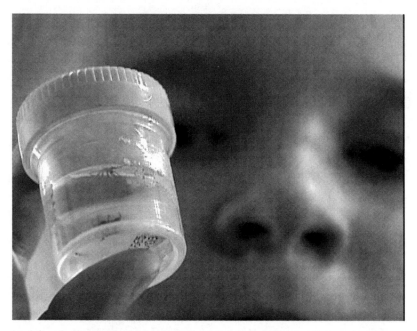

**Look for a backgrounds that lend a little context to the tight shot they surround.**

from your work. That's why it's a good idea to gather everything: a beginning (the accused entering), shots of the accused, his luckless attorney and he conferring about bail, cutaways of the Judge and District Attorney, a scowl from the accused, then a closing shot when he leaves. A few shots of the courtroom and some paper shuffling after the accused has left for good measure. That's enough for a package.

When you're assigned to be "pool cam" for drawn out events like courtrooms or funerals, set your time code for the time of day (in free run) and tell your reporter. They can log sound as it happens and perhaps gain advantage over reporters who wait until the end to log.

## Set Up

Where you set up is a crucial decision that should not be arrived at absently or because the other boys are setting up there. Ask yourself,

"Where's the light source? Where's the action? Where's the line?"

Generally speaking, shooting toward the sun will result in a blown out, too bright or blue background. Backlighting is the intentional choice of shooting towards the sun or key light, which requires you to fill with another light source or reflector. Having the sun at your back is usually easier.

Do not get stuck shooting toward a sunny window indoors using a (indoor) filter for artificial light. Subjects cast in a blue haze don't look good.

## Talking Heads

Though it will only comprise a fraction of any story or package, the talking head and how it fits into that story must be considered. Many interviews are tossed off by miking up the subject, stepping back and firing away. In fairness, some interviews will have to take place very quickly for a myriad of reasons, including overcoming reluctance of the subject, a tight deadline or any condition that forces a crew to hurry up and get the interview. But even when time is tight, photojournalists must consider how the interview is going to look in editing.

Place your subject in light that is flattering. Direct sunlight is usually too bright, causes squinting and shiny faces. Not enough light and you lose facial details. The easiest location to find in a hurry is outside and in the shade. Turn the subject so the background has, at least, partial shade. A sunny background behind a subject in the shade is usually blown out.

Indoor lighting that's quick and looks good on TV requires different considerations and has its own set of traps. Overhead fluorescent lights make women look like Dusty Springfield. Raccoon eyes. Better to use the ceiling light for a backlight. The battery light or lights you set up should be your main source or key light.

Office interviews are deadly because subjects sitting next to a wall blend into the background. You want a background that's out-of-focus, blurry. That gives three-dimensionality within the frame. Position subjects as near the center of the room as possible then set the camera as far away as you can. Commodious offices have better spacing and usually look better in interviews.

The pinnacle of interview background or foreground has a recognizable part of the story in the frame, but slightly out of focus. If the subject is talking about a family member, position the subject so their relative is behind them and a little blurry. In this way, you add to the story you're telling beyond the sound spoken by the talking head.

Every interview need not be shot tight with a blurry background. Some interviews are better shot wide. Everything is in focus, so make sure it has a few qualities going for it. I shoot interviews wide if the subject is a "hand talker". If they are animated with their body, this energy can lend to the story beyond the words coming from their mouth.

**Foreground, even out-of-focus, can lend to the story in the back ground. Like the story of this high school principal who objected to a marigold peace sign planted in the campus turf. Most shots tell one aspect of a story. Two or more story elements in one shot is a story telling shot.**

When you shoot interviews wide, look for diagonal lines or circles that lend visual perspective. Position the camera on a tripod, desk or chair to take advantage of these lines. This makes the shot three dimensional and interesting visually.

## Is Your Video Blurry and Out of Focus?

Then you might need glasses.

Sometimes, we shoot out of focus b-roll (video covering track or soundbites) intentionally or blur b-roll in editing, using the "mosaic" feature (the effect that obscures part of the frame like a face or obscene hand gesture.) Before you shoot blurry video purposely or use the effect in editing, ask two questions.

Why am I blurring the image? Would a focused image with

a clear subject tell the story better? B-roll should be in focus and every shot should have a subject.

With interviews and a-roll, we are sometimes not allowed to show subject's faces. These people want privacy and usually for a good reason. We sometimes comply by blurring their face or not lighting them against a bright background which makes their face too dark to see. A too dark interview face is better because it still moves and shows emotion in the movement. Showing the subject's hands is also preferable to blurring their face. Hands demonstrate emotion.

Shadows carry emotional weight. Set up a light and shoot their profile in shadow against a wall. Or outside, positioning them near a wall with a shoulder toward the sun. Another alternative is looking over the subject's shoulder at the reporter, or on-lookers listening attentively.

The problem with blurry video is when we use it for stories that don't require it. Entire sections of a story are sometimes covered with blurry video. A vague picture of kids or cars or any shot purposely out of focus is not a story telling shot. Every shot needs a subject that moves the story. Never leave viewers wondering at what they should be looking.

## Cut Aways

In England, they call it a "noddy". It's shot behind the back of an interview subject with the reporter listening and occasionally nodding. A device, to be sure. But necessary to avoid jump cuts when sound bites are butted together.

Cut aways aren't rocket science or even very good story telling, but done poorly may distract. Position the camera behind the subject, avoid un-flattering "butt shots" and let it roll while the subject is speaking. In editing, match the cut away with the sound you're covering so they appear to fit.

Another cut away is a shot of the subject's hands moving. If the bite you cut to or away from is a medium shot including the subject's face and moving hands, it's possible to match hand movement. A seamless, elegant solution to jump cutting.

One cut away that works universally is stepping at least ten yards from the interview and shooting it wide. The subject and reporter take up two or three squares in a nine square R3 grid. Have the subject in the frame approximately where their face appears in the interview. That way viewers don't have to search the frame to find them coming into or out of the bite.

A poor cut away does not match the words that are spoken; the lip flap of the subject is off. It's distracting if the reporter's expression isn't consistent with the sound bite's emotion, like laughing at something serious.

## Good Opening Shots

If you get a good opening shot and know it, look for a closing shot that's similar and complementary. This can give a nice "book end" quality to the edited piece.

At a picnic for Hurricane Katrina survivors, I shot the park scene wide with a couple playing dominoes in the foreground. This was my opening shot. We did a few interviews and I went back and saw our best interview subject, Cynthia, sitting on a picnic table talking to some other survivors. For a closing shot, I went behind the domino board and shot Cynthia through it with the domino pieces in blurry foreground. This gave the package circularity: ending where it began. Except now you know the rest of the story, as they say. It also gave the reporter some action to write to for a snappy close.

Sometimes, falling back on cinematic convention can give a news story a good opening or close when nothing better presents itself. Subjects moving toward the camera, like the opening credits of a thousand movies and television shows, can provide a good place to start visually. It's not iconoclastic, but it may be the best opening shot you have.

**Look to create fortunate framing. Accidents like this occur more frequently when you antici-
pate where to put the camera lens.**

## Closing Shots

Good news writers save the most emphatic word or phrase for the
end of the paragraph. The best closing shots emphasize the story's
emotion. If a good ending isn't obvious, then go back to the story's
best interview subject, whoever that is, and remind viewers of them
and their story one last time.

End your story as emphatically as possible. A good ending
punctuates like an exclamation point or period. Cinematic convention works for closing shots also in the absence of something better.
A subject moving away from the camera, a la <u>Casablanca</u>, makes
sense visually and may be the best you have.

## Don't Be Married to Your Tripod

However nasty the implication in the title, photojournalists know
what we're talking about. It's liberating to pull your camera off

the sticks when a story is moving. Shooting from your shoulder at good action directly in front of you yields compelling pictures and sound. The same action shot twenty or even ten feet away with a camera mounted on a tripod isn't as interesting. Consider the Oswald assassination film or battlefield footage.

Hand held shots relate an out of control feel which can benefit some stories. It has the effect of transporting viewers temporarily. It brings the viewer from his couch into the center of the whirl. It's the juice, and works to deliver a feeling of what the place and situation were like at that moment.

Shooting off your shoulder from the middle of the action improves the look of ordinary stories, too—not just a protest.

Seeming mistakes can tell a story when you find a creative spot to use them. Running with a camera while it's recording produces shaky, noisy video and can be a very exciting shot and good natural sound when it fits the story.

## Do Fries Go with That Shake?

Shooting steady shots is a must for professional-looking stories.

"Rock solid" is how photojournalist Marc Anderson describes it. Wobbly, shaky or not quite steady video doesn't satisfy like rock steady pictures. At the same time, you have to know when to pull the camera off sticks and just go with the flow of what's happening during a story without worrying about perfect steadiness.

In order to shoot steady, one needs a solid tripod and tripod head. The latter can easily wobble or drift with pans and tilts. When a tripod isn't handy but I need to zoom in, I put the camera on the ground and shove my hand or foot under it. In a room or office, I put the camera on a table or steady it on a chair. Finally if I need to, I'll sit Indian fashion with the camera in my lap. Point, roll and hold my breath for ten seconds. Older photographers may want to try turning off their heart pacemakers for extra steadiness.

**Handheld photography often lends to the shot and story you create, like this Labrador shaking off a recent bath.**

## Depth of Field

TV news photojournalists can use an element of still photography to make their news stories look better. Strictly speaking, depth of field is the distance between the lens and whatever it is focused on—similar to focal length. Manipulating your focus so everything in focus and out of focus pertains to the story is using depth most effectively. Picture a slightly out of focus little girl playing in the foreground while the camera's subject, the mother, is in focus standing at the back of the hospital room watching her sick daughter. That's using depth of field to tell a story. Still photographers have a word for the much-appreciated out-of-focus portions of the frame. Bokeh. And generally speaking, more expensive lenses have smaller f-stops creating more bokeh.

Here are some other examples of good depth of field. A soldier leaving on another tour of Iraq may be interviewed with his duffel and name tag in the foreground slightly out-of-focus. Interviewing

the coach while the pitcher throws off the mound in the background adds something to the coach's words.

The macro adjustment gives depth of field to any shot focused on a very near subject. If the background pertains, that's good depth of field. Manipulating depth of field to cram action and story into the frame is good shootin'.

## Subjective Camera

Point of view is an occasional consideration for photojournalists. Our camera is an objective eye scanning the scene for details that may accurately inform viewers. Sometimes we use our camera subjectively to capture an image or moment as it might be seen by an individual in a news story. For instance, when events are happening quickly and the camera darts around like the heads and eyes of someone on the street, that is using a subjective camera.

A great example of using a subjective camera to tell a story is the 1947 Humphrey Bogart film, <u>Dark</u> <u>Passage</u>. He's just escaped from San Quentin Prison and is hiding out in San Francisco. The camera scans nervously whenever strangers enter the room. When nosy neighbor, Agnes Moorehead eyes Bogie suspiciously, the camera sees and intuits every sideways glance the way he sees it. The camera for the first half hour is Bogart and its lens sees through his eyes. This is not just film school stuff. Good photojournalism may include the subjective camera from time to time, if it helps tell the story and doesn't distract.

Out West, we have a growing population of mountain lions. We call them cougars. Cougars and people don't play well together, yet attacks from these big cats are increasingly common. If someone gets hurt, it makes the news. The trouble is, cougars are very elusive and one rarely even glimpses them outside a zoo setting.

The Oregon Department of Fish and Wildlife occasionally capture a bad cat, but that is virtually the only time people with cameras get near enough for pictures: a huge cat reclining in a tree waiting for a dart. So how do you tell the story of people attacked by a cougar? One way is to tell it subjectively, through the eyes of the cat. Hand hold the camera behind the bushes at knee level focused on the people near the house. That's a cougar's eye view or, as we refer to it, "cougar cam". It's a good shot, too. Throw an effect in there like "black and white" or "blur" or "sharpness" and it's works nicely.

A little kid got lost and wound up near the freeway. Pushing the camera through the bushes along the highway until it stopped where the traffic moved by was a good way of telling that boy's story. Subjective camera was the device.

## What's in Your Trick Bag?

 Watch your work with a critical eye. Critique stories alone in the edit bay and show them to co-workers whose stories strike you. Find the shots and sequences you particularly like. Pay attention to what others notice. That is likely what you have an eye for.

When you know what you like to shoot, look for it and put it in your stories. *Play to your strengths*. Whether hitting a baseball, applying makeup or shooting the lead story for five, this is a good strategy. It's the secret sauce of accomplished photojournalism.

Any story I'm assigned to, be it dynamic with a lot of action or just a meeting, I'll be looking for a few things. I like matched action sequences. They move a story better than anything else to my eye. I listen for sounds that tell the story and gather them loud and clean. I try to find a place in the finished piece for any unguarded human reaction or moment that relates to the story. I get a charge seeing them inside the eyepiece, on the monitor when I'm editing, and finally when the story airs. It's my style of shooting. Identify your style and use it to fit the story.

## My Blue Period

Out West, our summers are often punctuated by forest fires at the end of the season. Most stations cover the big fires burning within their viewing areas. For news people, fire stories can be a relief from the general assignment humdrum and newsroom politics. Plus, it gets you into some beautiful areas.

My entire career in TV news has been spent in the state of Oregon where we have some ripping fires. I will not go down the list of conflagrations, but I love covering fires. That sounds so wrong—to enjoy something with the potential to destroy homes, pretty landscape and occasionally lives. But smoke and the quality of light showing through it renders great pictures. Especially when the camera is white balanced correctly.

In 2003, we had a big fire out by Summer Lake in Lake County. A shallow, desert lake at the base of the Fremont National Forest, it dries up entirely in summer. That means there is no lake in summer at Summer Lake. The locals must appreciate this several thousand acre contradiction since the biggest event locally is the Mosquito Festival in Paisley when they celebrate that insect's appearance. Somebody out there has a sense of humor.

The fire had been reported but not covered by any TV news crews until it started threatening homes. I started early one Saturday in August driving that direction with a fairly new reporter. The area of homes in the fire's path was two hours south and east of Bend.

We arrived in time to shoot a little fire by the highway. Scrub juniper and sage brush crackled a few feet off the dirt with sweet, black smoke swirling above the flames. Fire crews worked their tired, sooty butts off to keep it from jumping the asphalt. They were successful. Good stuff—pictures and sound.

Our first hit was in less than an hour then live shots again at 6 and 11. We fed the insatiable beast all evening. Sometime that night, parked by a desolate highway in one of the most remote sections of the state, the question came up about sleeping accommodations.

As it turned out the last room in nearby Summer lake had been booked by (who else?) channel eight. Our motel was in Lakeview, an hour away.

We made the drive without incident, but arriving at a sketchy hotel in the middle of nowhere at one a. m. was a lousy end to the day. That we were expected to return to the live truck by seven the next morning, really took the fun out of it.

My bed was a couch under a window. Our room was just off the street. This dimly lit avenue off the main drag was the alternate route for big rigs driving between who knows where and God knows why. Barely a street light with a stop sign at the corner, the thundering exhale of jake brakes shuddered against the window every fifteen or thirty minutes as the big trucks decelerated coming into town. The couch was not uncomfortable, I kept reminding myself until the sun came up.

The next morning we stopped for a bottled ice coffee at the local Dumpy Mart. Back in the car, my reporter shook the concoction vigorously above her lap. Without warning, the lid flew off followed by half its creamy contents. Some spilled on my jeans, but mostly on hers. At that point my intrepid reporter earned a nickname.

Mocha.

Poor, little Mocha. She was fresher than I was at that station and wanting badly to graduate to the anchor desk. She did eventually advance to the position of weekend anchor before quitting and moving to India.

That second day in Summer Lake she was chomping at the bit to break some hard hitting fire story. And so was I. But the lack of sleep made it difficult to keep my stoke going.

Smelling vaguely of sour coffee, I was dragged around that day by a girl fifteen years my junior with an ambition burning harder than the bunch grass. I tried to keep up. We shot a few interviews with locals nervous about fire blowing their way. A couple members of the fire crew stopped long enough to give us some good sound and video of dusty boots and yellow nomex shirts streaked with charcoal and ash.

Arriving back at the truck to cut our story, I pushed my first tape into the player deck and felt a sickening thud in my stomach. I'd shot the entire day with my camera filter where I'd set it the night before: balanced for artificial light in the darkness at night. All that beautiful natural light the next day rendered my video bluer than Roy Orbison after a bad breakup.

It's possible to correct for bad color and the truck engineer, sensing my panic, assured me this could be worked out and not to worry. My reporter loved the story we had gathered that day, and could not be dissuaded from using my blue video. I asked her to use the highway fire from the day before. I should have insisted, begged even.

So she wrote it and I cut it. Not really happy with the blue video, I tried at several turns to correct for it. My engineer assured me that in the end, he could adjust the "chroma" to take all the blue out and it would look dull but not blue.

During this time, a violent electrical storm moved into the valley. Anyone familiar with wild land fires knows lightning storms are a mixed blessing. Occasionally, there is enough moisture to quench a fire and slow its destruction. But more often, the rain falls lightly to earth when it reaches that far. Lightning may spark new fires in places fire fighters have difficulty reaching. This is when fires become complexes: a multitude of fires burning away from and toward each other in unpredictable ways.

**Look out for that lightning, Danny. It'll turn your video blue.**

With this electrical storm came greater urgency for fire crews and a fresh wrinkle of pressure for television crews. The story was changing and the lightning was making it dangerous to be there. Our live truck engineer was concerned for his crew's safety. I was outside preparing for a live shot, hoping to avoid being vaporized by lightning.

After the live shot and trusting my story's color had been "corrected", I returned to the sat truck and out of the rain. The truck's satellite phone rang and the engineer grabbed it. It was for me.

"It's Mike." The news director.

"Oh, no", I said in my head and felt my mouth get squishy. This was going to be bad, so I retreated to the folly of positive thinking. I thought well maybe he just loved the story and was calling to tell us. Maybe getting struck by lightning will give you a perfectly even sun tan. I took the phone with my face just half un-unsquished.

"What happened with that story?! It was blue!!"

My brain reeled a little and my mouth wasn't moving right. I could only echo a small, poorly formed question.

"It was blue?"

Then to my surprise and gratitude, another reporter spoke up. He said seven words that were like a life raft under my sorry, blue butt.

"It looked fine when we fed it."

Again, I could only echo words I heard floating by, so I repeated these to Mike. And then I said something about the violent electrical storm bearing down on us. The suggestion being that the video was fine and the electrical storm must have turned my story blue somewhere between the satellite truck and the big bird in the stratosphere. Sure. It could happen.

So the news director asked to speak to the engineer who said he really couldn't talk because there was a huge electrical storm messing up his signal and we may have to move to another location and the satellite phone is breaking up. Major path issues. I couldn't believe what I was hearing. Or how happy I was. There's exhilaration, not getting in trouble when you might. Not as satisfying as performing a task well in the first place, but a good dose of adrenaline—with a pinch of nausea. Though it remains my Worst Day Ever at work, it was not without some upside.

Journalism students may not realize that one can learn a lot from their mistakes. And bring your game up further than by examining stories that came off great. But you can't be timid about reflecting on personal disaster. You've got to wade right in, smell the smells and be honest with yourself. You'll be a lot better off than by pretending you never make mistakes or worse, blaming your mistakes on others. That act becomes transparent in a hurry and co-workers will resent you for it.

This story illustrates how crazy this business can be at its worst (best?) I actually got some sleep that night and turned a pretty good package the next day. A small victory, as we say. I also got a pretty cool hat out of it.

# Light and Lighting

THE SUBJECT OF LIGHT IS THE SECOND MOST IMPORTANT PHOTOGRAPHIC consideration, after choosing the subject and before composition. For news, natural light outside and available light indoors are the norm. Good photojournalists use that light to its advantage by placing the subject in well lit spaces. Under-lit situations do not translate well to news. That's more a film domain, like film noir or horror movies.

A shadowy face may look expressive and beautiful in a still photograph, but translates less well to a television screen. Though the light is the same, the cameras reproduce it differently. Modern digital cameras can do amazing things in low light. But, as yet, there is no setting that renders under lit interviews into something that looks good on television.

Lighting for television involves manipulating existing light sources and augmenting them to render the most flattering, expressive subject. The object of good lighting for television has less to do with simulating the human eye than trying to use the camera to its strengths. Bright, focused images look good on television. Low light situations rarely look as good.

## Three Point Lighting

Good interview lighting emanates from three points. The key light is the strongest source and should light the side of the subject's face furthest from the camera. A fill light, less bright than the key light, should illuminate the near side of the face while allowing for shadows and detail in the eyes, cheeks and hair. The back light should be behind the subject on the same side as the camera. The back light should bring out a little detail in the hair and lend three-dimensionality (depth). That is classic three point lighting. The ideal.

## Artificial Light Sources

In broadcast quality cameras, artificial (indoor and street) light reproduces best when white balanced on filter one. These will have temperatures around 3.0, plus or minus .5. Once you get above 4.0 then the brightest daylight filter, three, may work better. You might encounter this at an indoor sports event or arena.

Sunlight often mixes with artificial light when it shines through a window. For good skin tones in these situations move your subject away from the sunlight and windows. Find a dominant light source that is artificial then white balance on filter one. Or just close the shades or blinds to eliminate the sunlight entirely. A little blue light may be interesting peeking between blinds behind the subject and out-of-focus. But as soon as that blue light intrudes on your subject's face or hair, it's distracting. If the sunlight is brighter than the indoor lights then go with the dominant light source. Turn off the room lights and white balance on a daylight filter, likely filter three.

## Natural Light

In full daylight, I pre-set the white balance on filter two. That said, I'm looking for my first opportunity to get a proper white/temperature balance. Then I "re-white".

Full sunlight looks fine on the pre-set. Subjects standing in the shade require a fresh white balance. Alongside the pre-set position on most cameras will be two other settings: A and B. With these one may obtain a color balance for full shade and another for sun/shade mix. Switch back and forth as the light dictates.

Use filter four for subjects lit by bright sunlight, reflected water or snow. This renders colors a little darker and richer than filters three or two. You may need to open the iris slightly to keep subjects from looking too dark.

Rainy days and low natural light look best on filter three. Because it's slightly brighter, you may need to close the iris in some situations to compensate. This filter works fine indoors with window sunlight as your key light. Another nice effect is using window light for a back light then "keying" with a blue gel or dichroic daylight filter. Obtain your white balance on filter three and it should look fine. But turn off any room lights. Any other artificial light in this situation will look brown.

## Night Video

 White balancing manually in artificial light can render

superior, truer looking video than the preset temperature of 3.2. The less light you have and lower white balance temperature, the greater the difference in the appearance of skin tones and colors. A few tenths of a point on filter two in broad daylight hardly effects how skin tones reproduce. Filter one, however, balanced for 2.9 can look vastly different than 3.2. I try to get the lowest temperature balance I can for artificial light. I'll tweak the iris to manipulate the number and get a lower temperature reading. I like the way it looks. After working nightside for years, you know what you like. I think a 2.7 or 2.8 renders realistic, less harshly lit street scenes. Sodium lights at 3.2 blast orange unnaturally. For live shots with sodium lights illuminating the background, put an amber gel over

the key light then white balance. This will remove the orange cast from the subject/talent and background.

The half hour before and after sunset is called the magic hour by photographers who appreciate soft, pretty light. Use filter three and white balance manually, expecting a temperature between 5.9 and 9.0. Between sunset and night, white balance on filter one with the subject lit by your battery light or other artificial light. The dusky sky turns a pretty blue in the background and can be aesthetically pleasing.

The important thing is to experiment and find the color balance you prefer for shooting at night. If you don't have a LCD screen in your camera, use the live truck monitors to test different white balances. You'll appreciate the subtle differences.

## Run and Gun

I leave my camera's white balance pre-set whenever we might have to run and gun. So I can grab the camera and start rolling. Be ready to jump out of the car and start shooting because this may be the best opportunity for pictures and natural sound. Always have a tape in your camera, or whatever format you shoot on. Do not leave yourself out of position or fumbling with tapes and buttons. That's strictly for amateurs.

Thinking ahead and being ready for something sudden is how professionals prepare.

## Using Available Light

Experienced photographers take advantage of available light, particularly for interviews and live shots. If there's an overhead artificial light, use it for a backlight by positioning your subject underneath and in front of it.

The best key light of all is the sun visible behind the clouds. Like a great heavenly filter, the consistent cloud cover we enjoy ten months out of the year in Oregon, usually works fine as a key light for outdoor interviews.

Live shots are a different animal with a different set of considerations. Using available light during daytime (aka the sun) is always a good choice, but not as the only light source. One needs to augment daylight live shots with fill and/or back lighting. Some of the different moves for wrestling this reptile, live shot lighting, are coming up.

## Backlighting

This is lighting favored by portrait photographers to get a nice glint off a subject's hair against an out-of-focus background. For news stand-ups and interviews, backlighting gives separation to a talking head from whatever is behind them. Usually when you backlight, photographers have to open the iris so the face is bright enough. This may cause the background to become over-exposed and "blown out". To compensate, we use a strong key light source like an HMI or strong reflector to illuminate the reporter's face and front. Then you close the iris for that subject and hopefully return some detail to the background.

As an available back light, full sunlight is not necessary. Sunlight peaking through a shade tree is a perfectly bright backlight and won't require such a strong key light to compensate.

## Live Shots

Live shots need to look good. For yourself, your crew, viewers and producers in the booth, it's imperative the live shot is lit properly. A reporter standing in too bright sunlight or dark shade is the definition of small-market live shots.

Set up your lights and tripod ahead of time, in case you move up in the show or editing goes overlong.

In sunny conditions, I like to move my reporter into a shady spot and key with a bright, strong light source like an HMI, which I can adjust. That way the reporter is as bright as the background. The standard for network live shots during the day is three point lighting on a reporter in full shade. Sometimes that shade is created by a screen. You don't see reporters standing in full sunlight on CNN, unless it's a stand up or breaking news situation.

Stand far enough away from the truck, so the microphone doesn't pick up generator hum.

Pull the interview subject or reporter far enough away from the background to render some depth of field and separation.

Sand bag your light stands. Keep any shadows the lights create off the reporter and out of the frame.

In the minutes leading up to a live shot, have the test rack or live truck engineer look at your white balance, iris and audio level.

In some breaking news situations, there won't be time to find a shady live shot location, let alone set up lights. If this is what you're stuck with, make the best of it and use a reflector to fill the shady side of a reporter's face. It may not be perfect but it looks better than a "Lisa Bright and Dark" countenance.

Another way to spruce up an evening live shot in the rain or snow is positioning your car headlights behind the reporter and out of frame. Besides functioning as a backlight, the effect causes the precipitation to show up better and gives the impression it's falling heavier than it is.

## Adjust the Iris for the Background

When lighting a live shot or interview, find the background you want, set the iris for it and leave it there. Next, light your subject manipulating the key light, but don't touch the iris again. This way both subject and background will be bright enough. It may seem counterintuitive. But if you light your subject first and set the iris for that situation, the background will likely be over or under lit.

# How Is Sound Like Breathing?

IF YOU'RE NOT BREATHING, YOU'RE IN A LOT OF TROUBLE. YET YOU RARELY hear anyone express much appreciation for it.

"Done any good breathing lately?"

Natural sound is critical to good story telling. But it's often a secondary consideration. When it's used to emphasize an aspect of the story or a person in it, natural sound leaves a strong impression. Creative use of natural sound can breathe life into a package that's rushed and breathless and tell a story as effectively as any picture, interview sound or track.

## Layering Sound

Underneath a-roll sound (reporter track and bites), there should be a consistent layer of b-roll sound that occasionally pops up inside and between the a-roll. Recognize good natural sound and find ways to fit it in. You may want to begin with the sound of the birds up full for a few seconds before the bite. Or you may break the bite into two parts covering the first section with bird video and insert the bird sounds up full before the talking head appears, whichever works to the story's advantage.

Any surprise with b-roll or natural sound is better than sound you expect. Natural sound that intrudes a little on track and bites is fine, but not when the former makes hearing a-roll difficult. Natural sound works to full advantage in spaces you create for it.

## The Power of Three

An effective way to present good, natural sound is to use three bits of natural sound consecutively. It may be the same sound heard three times. Most effective are three distinct sounds one after the other. A group of rafters preparing for their float trip rip the Velcro on their booties, snap the buckle of the life vest and then sploosh the oar into the water as they paddle off. RRRRIP! SNAP! SPLOOSH! That's a nice break from a reporter's track or sound bite, and it hastens the pace.

## Silence

Look for a strong memorable image and allow an absence of audio for a second or two as the picture rolls out. This lends resonance and depth by bringing a viewer where they can look at something and consider it. But if there's no sound, won't viewers change the channel? Not if the story is compelling, and the image dynamic.

## Lavaliere Microphones Gather the Most Interesting Sound

A few sound-gathering habits bring interesting, story telling sound to a piece. For one, you don't do anything at all. Just leave your lavaliere microphone on a subject after the main interview and step back. This is the microphone we pin on subject's lapels. It's unobtrusive. People forget it's there and when they do, they loosen up and often say the most interesting things when the camera seemingly departs. I step back and busy myself shooting cutaways, but keep it wide on the reporter and subject, rolling if the latter is letting loose with something juicy. Or zoom in if the light is still good. Get some depth of field. Sometimes it looks better than the formal interview. Nothing disingenuous here. You're in a setting with a camera, microphone, reporter. . . Anything you say can and will be used to make the story better.

The lav can also be used to gather natural sound. Find a subject doing something that pertains to your story and pin the lav mike on them. Shortly, they'll forget the mike's attached and everything they say is being recorded. They'll get into whatever they're doing. In the process, you may gather a piece of sound or off-hand comment that comes in handy later. In logging and editing, look for this clean, interesting sound to change the pace in a story.

## Clean Audio

Audio may seem simpler to gather than color balance, but it's more often a problem. Less than perfect audio is just as distracting as weird color. And while a color balance can be fixed with most editing software, bad audio is more difficult to clean up. Interview and natural sound can have a myriad of problems: too low, too hot, radio frequency interference and so on.

Is your audio signal microphone or line level? If the microphone is hard-wired directly to the camera, it's "mike level". If you're taking sound from an external source (i. e. a multiplier or "mult box"), know whether the audio is coming from the box at mike or line level. Having your camera set for one when it's the other will render the audio unusable, either too "hot" or inaudible. Whenever I plug the cube into any mult box, I set the box audio to microphone level and record it that way. If it's too quiet or non-existent only then do I change the setting to line level. The issue arises at press conferences, concerts, the state legislature, staged events and so on. Use a "pad" for hot, line-level audio coming from multiplier boxes. Mine is 50db and brings that over-modulated, city council sound down to a clean, usable level.

Employ the stick microphone whenever crowd, traffic, machine noise intrudes on interview sound. If it's quiet, the lavaliere works great and is less visually distracting. In windy conditions, a lav tucked between a shirt and jacket may pick up interview sound better than a stick microphone held out in the wind.

## Bad Sounds

An automobile driving by may be worth a one second "nat pop", but the sound of an engine idling is strictly sound under. You have to use your own discretion. Generator hum is annoying when you bring it up full. So is an air conditioner, wind noise, leaf blowers. What about the buzz in a fluorescent light? Some sound needs to be sold. Fluorescent light buzz can work if a hand flips a switch (action) and the light turns on with a buzz (reaction.) Use your discretion. I used the click of an air conditioner turning on for a story about increasing energy bills. The machine's hum made sense later in the piece. Crowd noise is exciting when it matches a visual moment. There aren't hard and fast rules about bad audio. The question is, does this piece of sound lend to the story or distract?

## Microphones

There is a universe of microphones out there. Enough to fill a book. A few are suitable for news-gathering. For the most part these are **omni-directional** microphones: the hand-held variety for "man on the street" interviews. These get clamped into a stand for press conferences. They're handy in changing situations where subjects move around or interviewing several people at once. These microphones gather sound from every direction but the loudest will be whatever is closest to the microphone. The drawback is that omni-directional microphones will pick up any sound that's present.

**Uni-directional** microphones should point toward the subject with the rear of the mike pointing toward undesirable sound. Their news application is minimal.

**Lavaliere** microphones are the clip-on types you see in sit down interviews. They are also useful gathering natural sound. Because they are fixed to the subject's shirt or collar, typically eight inches from the chin, they may not be moved when other undesirable sound pops up. When this is the case, get out the hand-held microphone and have the reporter hold it a few inches from the subject's chin then adjust your audio levels.

The microphone fixed to your camera is called a **shotgun** or camera microphone. These are omni-directional and not really great for anything but b-roll sound. I replaced mine long ago with a **Sennheiser** XY attached by a curly cord. It's powered by a AA battery and works like a champ. I prefer it because the audio is loud, clean and works in a pinch for man-on-the-street interviews or whenever we're working fast.

## Windscreens

These pull their weight in windy conditions. Inside, they don't do much. Our radio colleagues, who are acutely tuned in to audio quality, frequently remove windscreens for indoor press conferences and interviews.

In inclement weather, a foam windscreen absorbs a lot of moisture. It's always a good idea to remove it, wring out the water and leave it to dry. Otherwise, it can damage a microphone's internal parts.

The "dead cat" windscreen is preferred by some. It works fine, but must be kept out of the frame because it's distracting. I prefer foam for any hand-held or on-board type microphone that might find its way into the frame during an interview.

## The Invisible Stick Mike

An interesting way to gather MOS sound is using your reporter's back to hide a hand held microphone in a two shot. The reporter and interviewee appear to be standing on the street just talking.

It's feels like eavesdropping, cuts nicely to wide or tight shots and there's no distracting microphone flag hanging out there.

Of course, you can just pin a lav on the subject, step away and shoot it the same way. But you lose some spontaneity in the pinning. Merely walking up to someone and talking to them often elicits more honest talk.

It is difficult keeping reporters from standing in profile to the lens with the microphone protruding. This is not as interesting to look at as the invisible stick mike interview, though obviously it doesn't change the answers people will give.

## Microphone Aesthetics

The best looking microphone is one you can't see, but produces good audio. No microphone wires should be visible, hanging from a lapel or stretching over the shoulder. The mike should be pinned

An audio arsenal. Top to bottom: Lectrosonics UM400 (also known as a "lav mic"), Sennheiser MD46 (stick microphone), Sennheiser XY with curly cord (camera or "on board mic"), Sennheiser SKP3000 cube (aka a "butt plug".)

as unobtrusively as possible, eight inches or so from the chin on the lapel nearest the reporter. Photojournalists who strongly consider placement and visibility of microphones go so far as to pin a lavaliere inside a neck tie, so no microphone is visible. This can be advantageous in windy outdoor situations, too.

Absolutely avoid hand holding the lavaliere. Pinched between a thumb and forefinger, you get a lot of noise and rumble. Besides, it looks ridiculous.

Bright, station graphics are distracting for a reason—to leave an impression, hopefully. They look great on the side of a live truck or spinning around in some on-air promotion or graphic. But positioned under the chin of an interview subject, those same graphics can be a little loud and distracting. Zoom in tight enough to keep the microphone below the frame. A two shot with the cube visible is not a big deal. Any press conference with the usual phalanx of microphones, flags and cables cannot be controlled, so microphones will be visible in any wide shot of the podium. Use the wide shot for a cutaway, an opening or closing shot of the subject either walking in or leaving. For the most important sound bites however, shoot the speaker tight enough so the microphone orgy doesn't appear. This is sometimes impossible, particularly when you have more than one person speaking. It is normal to have the microphone flag at the bottom of the frame during live shots, even when the identical graphic is present on a cap, jacket, superimposed banner or even all four at once.

# Editing

HOW YOU SHOOT IN THE FIELD IS CRITICAL TO MAKING THAT STORY SING when it airs. Once it is shot though, it's no less important how those shots are ordered, their length and the sound that pops up around the bites and track.

## Pace and Flow

You've been handed the script for a minute and a half package. Now, you have an hour, if you're lucky, to cut it. Likely the writer was trying to keep the facts straight, saving a few choice words and phrases to bring the point home and create a little drama. It's not likely much consideration was given to the pace or flow of the final edited piece. Were it, your job would be easy. With script in hand, editors should look to create two things, pace and flow.

Pacing a story is usually left to the last person to shape it: the editor. It's the rhythm you control with the length of your shots. Shorter edits hasten the feel. The natural sound editors inject and bring up full around the a-roll slows things down and allows stories to breath. Matching action also picks up the pace.

Flow is pictures fitting the words in the script without too much starting and stopping. One shot moves into the next, one sequence after another without the feeling of interruption. Matched action creates flow. Backing up natural sound or b-roll into the end of the sound bite or the beginning erases the start/stop feel and lends flow.

For your first shot, don't beguile at the outset or begin a package with a too quick sequence. You'll lose viewers. Start with a good shot, easily understood but leading into the story to follow. Leave it up long enough for an uninformed viewer to see exactly what it is. After your first emblematic shot, you can use that sequence.

Leading up to your first really good sound bite, use shots of decreasing length. Cover the first second or two of a talking head. Leave that talking head up long enough for the director to key in the super-imposition (name and job title). Generally, six seconds is enough.

Even if your reporter didn't think about pacing, her voice track will tell you what your best choices will be. If you shot the story you are editing, close your eyes and listen to the voice track. Your mind's eye will project many of the pictures that fit the script.

If you've got one good shot with a lot happening and the shot lasts five or six seconds, place several quick shots before to pace it. Shots longer than seven or eight seconds are a little too long for a minute and a half package.

Where's the best spot for that matched action sequence? That will give flow wherever you put it. Leave the payoff shot a little longer than the shots that set it up.

Maintain the flow during long sound bites by covering the front and/or back with video. Allow some natural sound to come up full before showing the picture that goes with that sound. If the subject stops talking after the bite, leave them up for a second and a half into the next track. These devices smooth the intersections between track and bites, creating flow.

The best last shots last pretty long—at least three seconds. They don't have to be the longest shot in the story, but the best play out with the track or closing bite. Look for a shot that punctuates the emotion in the story. That's memorable.

Foreshadowing the last shot gives it greater impact. Realistically, that means showing the first few seconds of the last shot a little earlier in the story. You might foreshadow with a shot of a nurse pushing the gurney. Then for a closing shot, the patient is wheeled through the doors as the track ends. The best last shots reveal something you've been waiting for, however small.

Editing scripts which pay scant attention to pacing or video is sometimes referred to as turd polishing. Even a dashed off script can be improved in editing by marrying words and pictures.

OK, now. Hold on there, Buster. I believe reporters are initially responsible for the pacing of the story—at least setting a roadmap for it. I think in terms of nats, short bites, timing as I'm writing. That's why I log that stuff. That's part of how I chose my words and phrases. And that's why you'll see me mumbling to myself as I write. I put the rough polish on the turd, you finish it with a shiny one.

Writers should be tough on themselves. Edit ruthlessly words and phrases which don't add information or move the story. When writers look hard to remove the chaff, the story usually benefits.

## Track Back

With a voice track covered by strong corresponding b-roll video, you may create a little flow starting the video a few frames early. Not every edit. This smoothes the story out by losing some chunkiness. You want to avoid sound and pictures feeling like they stop and start, then stop and start again.

## Straight Cuts

There will be other places in the story where you want precise rhythm. Sound and pictures landing all-at-once gives a piece crispness, spontaneity and movement.

With good emphatic bites, you want to start everything from a straight cut. If you're fortunate enough to have an interesting shot with good natural sound, it is advantageous to begin them both at the first frame with sound up full and create a Moment.

## First, Last and Best Shots

When you meet someone for the first time, your first impression has a weight to it that diminishes as the meeting continues. The end of the conversation has a different significance than what came before. And so it is with your minute and a half story about the contentious school board meeting. The first shot must be visually arresting in order to keep the audience's finger off that pesky remote. Maybe your first shot is your best shot. Fine. But make sure it informs immediately about the story to come. Nothing confusing or too crowded to find the subject. If you know what your best picture is and where you want to use it, tell your reporter. Reporters want input about pictures and where to use them effectively.

Good endings include, but are not confined to, the story subject walking away. You might also go back to another tearful shot of the mother. Or a long embrace. Maybe you and your reporter were smart and chose to "book end" the package with a similar shot first and last. Or by using a continuation of the first shot for your last. Never leave yourself without a closing shot. Look for it when you're shooting. A lousy ending is like a cold French fry.

The best movie endings are more than people walking away or a camera moving away from the scene. In the movie, <u>Casablanca</u>, Rick and the Inspector walk away from the camera as it moves away, but the dialog is something like this:

"This is the beginning of a beautiful friendship." Beginning as ending.

And in <u>Sideways</u>, the last shot is a knock on the door. Another beginning.

Here's one that worked. The story slug was "Cancer Race". The opening shot was a breast cancer survivor looking physically tired, but happy to be in the last stretch of the race. We used a little sound from her and her daughter during the story. For a closing shot we went back to the survivor crossing the finish line. Her family applauded her effort and embraced her. A little reward at the story's end, tension released and a nice circularity.

Denouement is a perfect ending that reveals the conclusion to a series of events. Like the grandmother protesting outside an army recruitment office being taken away in a police car.

## Hold Back a Surprise

You don't have to lay all your cards on the table before you've played your hand. If you've got a surprise or unexpected detail, spring it on the viewer somewhere down the line. Like a "plot point" in movie writing. The story pivots around it and changes a little bit after. In news, it helps pick up the pace and gives viewers an "A-Ha!" moment; they feel something special has been revealed to them.

## Non-Linear Editing

If you're using a computer to store and edit video, we call that non-linear editing. We take it for granted now. But for TV news photojournalists, it's the best thing ever. Cameras improve incrementally as digital technology advances, but the jump between tape to tape editing and good non-linear software is huge. We move tracks around to insert sound, correct color, create effects and deliver our pictures with a few mouse clicks. It is a great leap forward. And no one's looking back. Some technologies, like music reproduction on vinyl record albums, have a quality we appreciate. Film photography and dark room technique still produce beautiful pictures. Shooting and editing tape is inferior to digital technology in virtually every way that matters in our business.

There is one small disadvantage to non-linear editing. When you get frustrated in the edit bay, there are no beta tapes to throw against the wall. Pounding the space bar doesn't feel as good as the sound of plastic exploding and may give you carpal tunnel syndrome.

## Avoiding Jump Cuts

When a person is standing here in one shot and there the next, your brain recognizes the inconsistency. One cannot be two places at once. It gets your attention though. That's why jump cuts, usually considered an editing mistake, are used intentionally in advertising, music videos and movies. Jump cuts aren't so much a mistake as they are a device.

When we present the news, viewers want to see and hear what actually happened. Not an interpretation. So this device rarely gets packed into the photojournalist's trick bag. There are exceptions. I've seen some creative reporter stand-ups that used jump cuts. And occasionally in longer pieces, a purposeful jump cut may help tell the story. For example, a crowded school ground cut to it empty of children. In these cases, editors use the jump cut intentionally.

If a jump cut finds its way in there accidentally, it's usually going to look like a mistake.

Avoiding jump cuts is easy. Getting from one shot to the other will work if you insert a close up between them. That is the best way to avoid a jump cut. Two less effective techniques are inserting a few frames of white between shots or dissolving. *If you can't solve it, dissolve it.* That's a joke. Neither the white frames or dissolve is a good option because neither has story telling value. The close-up should.

## Transititions

Editing is about transitions and considering the next shot to lay in. Look for the smoothest, most compelling shot that relates to the previous one. The best way to arrive at this decision is to shoot it that way in the first place. In the field as you gather video, select shots that edit together nicely. This is also called "in camera editing". It makes it easier for editors to work from your raw video, too.

The most common device for editing in camera is shooting a wide shot then a medium and finally a tight or super tight shot. You may also have the opportunity to shoot action and a complimentary reaction shot of someone watching the action. Always story telling. Matching action shots into a sequence of continuous movement edit together nicely. Into frame and out of frame shots fit most places and are right for beginnings and endings. Moments stand alone, but should be saved for maximum story telling impact. Super tight shots fit between virtually any two shots.

## Appropriate Use of Effects

Any time you change the original look of your video in the final edited piece, it is an effect. These should be used sparingly because manipulating or changing a picture alters the truth of the moment. We should not alter it even slightly without some consideration.

Amazing things can be done to correct color video after you've shot it. There is no excuse for blue video any longer. Correcting color and white balancing in editing is the only effect an editor should render without thinking about having changed the truth of the moment. Altering color balance for effect should only be done to tell the story better. For instance, a story about teens using their parent's prescription pills benefited from one sequence where the color balance of a party and scene of kids dancing was manipulated.

Any other computer generated manipulation of the original picture should pass the "truthiness" test.

Does this effect change the truth of the moment in the video as it was shot? Does it enhance it or dilute it or change it any way? If it doesn't, then it passes the test. If it does alter the moment, you've stepped onto "truthiness" turf. Avoid this real estate when you edit stories for TV news. Slow motion or zooms created in

editing are about the only other effects besides an improved color balance that are acceptable whenever you use them.

A dissolve should only be used in place of a straight cut where it's advantageous to the story. Straight cuts move and pace better. It's hard to improve upon a straight cut for telling a story. Dissolves appear more "professional" to some in our business because in the days of tape they were achieved by a fairly laborious "A-B roll". They have a tendency to impress the uninitiated and anyone who believes dissolves look more "network". Dissolves are only appropriate where it aids in story telling. For instance, sound from an interview subject may be covered with video pertaining to that sound. A dissolve from interview subject to video works nicely. Dissolves into and out of pre-produced pictures like mug shots or maps make the transition less jarring.

There are a few other situations where dissolves work, but many where they do not. We discussed using straight cuts in ever decreasing duration before your best long sound bite. A dissolve here would not work because it dulls crisp pacing and weakens the release of tension that pacing sets up. Try it both ways to gain an appreciation of straight cuts.

Dissolves have no place in matched action or sequences. Too frequent use of dissolves also hampers editors who have to cut a new story from your old one. Dissolves allow less shot on either end to be used in a re-edited story.

Dissolves are popular with the longer format pieces where a montage of images that evokes whatever the script is relating. But this is more "60 Minutes" terrain than your minute and a half package.

Editing software for news usually allows for slowing down or speeding up video. Video that's sped up or slowed down should be judged by one rule. Does it distract from or lend to the story being told?

In re-telling newsworthy events for television, viewers want facts and real pictures of the event. Whenever we deviate from that, we slip toward subjectivity, spin and truthiness.

Lastly, putting a fresh color balance on an interview whose color isn't quite true is always a good move. It's easy with non-linear editing software. There's no excuse for bad color balances anymore, but especially with interviews and a-roll sound.

## Keep It Tight

In editing, tightness lends flow, creates tension. But know where to let it breath and relieve a little tension. Tight at the beginning, as a rule. After that find the best place for a pause, a second or two of natural sound or reaction that gives pace. Even the most fast-paced stories need to breath in places.

## Breathing Life Into a Package

Many package-length stories are written without a pause or breath between the voice track and a-roll sound. Edited as written this makes stories that sounds hurried, tense and fairly in your face. People don't talk that way. It is doubtful viewers want to receive news this way, either.

We speak to each other with pauses, breaths, thoughtful gaps as we search for the right words. That is how we are used to hearing information presented orally. How can you add that naturalness to a minute and a half story without making it take twice as long? Let it breath. Voice track should not have introduced pauses, but if a picture is playing out in a visual way that tells the story, you can wait a few beats to bring in the track. Sound-bites frequently begin or end with the speaker taking a breath. Occasionally, edit in the breath, unless you're covering the bite. The same goes for verbal pauses. A "Hmmm" or a "Well. . ." all serve to let a story breath a little, give it some looseness and momentarily slow the pace a notch.

Some reporters want a breathless feel to stories. Hard news stories, in particular, are well served by fast pacing. But even these need a pause before a tearful witness or while a cop admits it's the worst thing he's ever seen. Every story benefits from pacing. It is often the empty spaces of a wheeze or sniffle that put an exclamation point on the story. Like the pauses in a Miles Davis ballad. The silence between notes is interesting. Similarly, the spoken word benefits from pauses. If you've paced a story fast up to a point, viewers are waiting for a breath.

The goal is to create some naturalness in the flow of sound. Another way to do it is to lay down your b-roll audio like a bed under the a-roll. Insert b-roll pops of natural sound when the a-roll is quiet or create gaps in the a-roll by stretching it out, and fill those gaps from the b-roll bed.

Natural sound opens things up while informing. The sound of footsteps, a creaky door or just some off-hand comment leading up to the picture improves pacing.

Read the script aloud before you begin editing. The words on the page will tell you where a pause belongs or does not. And the same script will read briskly in sections where the pace should be quick. These few minutes of preparation will help editors avoid the panic ten minutes before slot, wondering where to put in some "nats".

While you are editing b-roll sound, listen for good sounds that lend to the story and if you can break up the track or bite, inject that sound up full for a second. It usually fits perfectly. Never make the b-roll sound so loud that a-roll is difficult to hear. Any b-roll sound so good you want to raise it to the level of the a-roll is crying out for a natural sound break.

Good writers inject their stories with lots of natural sound. Always with an ear for where the sound fits best and adds to the story. This is not the same as writers who instruct editors to "put in some nats."

## Written Into a Hole

When you need to use too many cut aways or video that doesn't fit well, editors call this being written into a hole. This is when there's no appropriate video to match the words in a script. It doesn't have to be written this way. A phrase early in the script may give some context to otherwise weak video.

Police kept onlookers well back. . .

The hospital did not comment. . .

The scene had been cleared. . .

Any of the above make unexciting pictures fit better because they explain in the beginning why you're not seeing the event the script describes. A few well-chosen words early in the story keep editors out of holes by giving maximum meaning to the video, however poor. If a script is full of holes, ask the writer a question.

"What video were you thinking of to cover this section?"

If you're lucky, they know something you don't about the script or the whereabouts of some other video. If you're unlucky, you may get this response: "Just do your best."

All writers can do is their best with video poor stories. Sometimes writers have no choice. Case in point: a recent story where middle school students had been suspended. A few were arrested for a protest they held. The controversy concerned the punishment the students received and whether it was too severe. The problem is the protest happened three weeks earlier and we had no video of it. We also had no video of the incident at a track meet which prompted the protest. We had no access to the kids involved. So what do you do, short of giving up? We interviewed the district and some parents picking up kids willing to voice an opinion. We got shots of the school, the school sign, school buses, kids at a distance on the playground. The story used this video while I described a protest, the punishment, etc. Not ideal, but sometimes you have no choice. And yes, this was a story out of the newspaper assigned to me. A producer badly wanted it for his show, so we did what we had to do. In our script, I used a few choice phrases to put the story in context and to match the available video. In this case, it started something like, "the kids at school are calmed down now, but it was on this track at a recent meet...." You get the idea.

## Editing a Vosot

Everyone in this business, including J-school students at some point during their internship or first job, ask a co-worker,
"What's a vosot?"

There are no small jobs when it comes to what airs during the news. The term vosot is an acronym for *voice over sound on tape.* Vosots comprise the majority of local TV and national news stories. They are the type where the anchor or reporter reads a script live alongside the pictures that have been edited to fit. That's the "v. o." The sound on tape is the sound bite/talking head that comes after. After the sound bite, there is usually more v. o. and the anchor reading alongside those pictures.

Common, underappreciated and often dashed off in editing, there's a way to edit vosots correctly and avoid the cardinal error in these stories: flash frames before the sound bite and at the end of the trailing v.o. Flash frames are the very brief, sometimes just one frame (1/30 of a second) shots which occur just before the sound bite and talking head or the anchor appears after the trailing v. o.

Whatever the story, always show a wide shot of the scene early in the v. o. Know the full running length of the v. o. by reading the script aloud while timing it. When you lay in the last shot before the sound bite, start it three seconds before the bite and have it last, at least, five seconds after the bite is timed to commence. An eight second shot that starts a few seconds before the sound bite will avoid flash frames when read rates lag. Likewise, after the bite, editors should hold for eight or ten seconds, the last shot of v. o. before the anchor or reporter's face pops up. A few frames of a shot you can't make out or would like to see longer, is distracting. They are the most common editing mistake in TV news. And completely avoidable by holding your last shot.

# Confessions of a Live Shot Monkey

I have a new perspective on live shots after being relegated for almost two years to the morning (and noon) shows. We are 90% of the time "live for live's sake". I'm picturing myself just a few days ago, standing outside a courthouse at five a. m., reporting on a murder case with a plea deal and possible sentencing. That none of the participants of this trial were even awake yet did not discourage our ardor. Later that afternoon I reported live from the same spot several hours after everyone had gone home. Rarely is live television used to show something actually happening unless it's a natural disaster, drawn-out SWAT raid or Christmas shopping in progress. It's unfortunate, because live reporting at dynamic events is at least interesting and sometimes fascinating when events play out on screen in unpredictable ways. The rest of this standing in front of buildings or bushes, police or train stations reading a script is boring, and not very rewarding for viewers either.

Just a word of warning. We say it takes some passion to be driven in this TV news world. But these gratuitous, redundant live shots can kill that passion. The banality of being live at a location where everything has finished and everyone gone home except you is embarrassing and bad for morale of field crews. This, coming from a trained (and pretty good) live shot monkey.

## A Well Rested Monkey Is a Happy Monkey

I am, through the wisdom of new and better management, back to dayside reporting, Monday through Friday. In fact my new boss seems to really appreciate my story telling, as well as my live shot competence. Brighter days are here. I am having some good and rewarding days, along with the mundane and downright nasty ones, too. And I have a year and a half of constant live shot work that, looking back, may be an asset of experience. What's that saying, "if it doesn't kill you…"

## Team Coverage, Triple Boxes and All That Crap

When anchors read, "We have Live Team Coverage", producers squirm in their seats. They love this stuff. It's the sound of it. The big production value of a fancy graphic with anchors and reporters all on the screen together, sends them over the edge. It demonstrates horsepower and gives viewers the impression we are dominating an important story, so they'd better watch. Sometimes it is warranted. More often, it is hype and bravado. But that's TV news. If you've got it, flaunt it. I have to admit, as a reporter it is a bit of a rush to be in the team coverage triple box (or quad box or higher) and hear the team coverage battle cry. Especially, if you're going first.

"We have live team coverage of the flooding. But first. the most important part of the story from our top reporter, Tim Gordon."

Wow, that feels good just writing it. Ego.

There are plenty of times when it's simply too much. Today, I did a story about commuting to work by bus to beat the high cost of gasoline. I decided to become a bus commuter. The story followed my ride and included others on the bus as well. It documented a positive experience on a commuter bus line out of county. But they lumped me in with a random assault story that occurred on a metro bus line so they could create Team Coverage. Two different stories. Two different bus services. But, oh my God, we have a chance for team coverage.

Late in the day and not long before air time, I learned what was coming and I balked, raising my concern to the producer, but to no avail. (Fortunately, a technical glitch kept me out of a triple box with the bus violence reporter.) I did have to be live in a pre-show segment following mention of the bus violence story. I said:

"And I'm Tim Gordon with a peaceful story of a mass transit commute. Why I'm riding the bus along with many other new riders, coming up."

Sometimes you can't change the system, but you can tweak it a little. I love team coverage when it's real. Otherwise, it's just a blustering, big noise. This is how Chicken Little would deliver his message were he a producer.

## Live Shots Benefit from a Stick Mike

This is so because reporters can move it nearer their voice to avoid distracting background noise, like traffic or people shouting. The mike flag keeps everyone happy upstairs. The only time a lavaliere microphone should be substituted is to keep the reporter's hands free to handle a prop or excessive scripts/laptops etc. In almost every other situation a hard-wired, stick mike is the best choice.

## Use Fresh Batteries

Ever heard a reporter's microphone start over-modulating then cut out on a live shot? How about the reporter who mysteriously goes to black? I saw a silent reporter lip flapping on CNN last week. That's live TV! Bad live TV. These embarrassing mistakes can be avoided by replacing old batteries with fresh ones. Unless you enjoy being asked to go straight to the news director's office, it's easier to pop in a fresh 9 volt and charged camera brick before the live shot starts.

## Hard Wire in Emergencies

A ghost in the machine of live TV is lousy live shot sound. The dreaded gremlin. Remote microphones with cubes and lavaliere can be capricious. Weak batteries, signal interference, bad connections. Whatever the problem may be, if the live shot is a minute away and the producer's screaming about audio? Two words. Hard wire. Keep 20 feet of good audio cable in your fanny pack all the time for this circumstance and any other that requires quick, clean audio.

Hard wiring sends an audio signal to the truck at microphone level. So keep the engineer abreast of last minute changes. It could save your life or at least keep a producer from jumping down your throat when you get back to the station.

Hard wiring your live shot when it's not an emergency is a good idea, too. If the live shot is static and the reporter's "mark" is five to ten feet in front of the camera then hard wire your audio in the first place. Spare yourself and everyone else last-minute heart palpitations.

## Change Live Shot Backgrounds

Move your reporter slightly from show to show for live shots. That way the background may change and shots don't look identical. This is sometimes impossible as when every station's reporters are in a chum line and there's no room to move. But when you can adjust, give yourself a different background, however slightly. Viewers get bored if they think they are seeing the exact same story twice.

## Swimming Upriver with the Tuna

A live shot that shows something interesting or sets up your piece especially well, is a thing of real TV beauty. When you have that, it feels like you nailed a perfect dive in the Olympics. Of course, breaking news requires live shots. Some of our best work can be done there and in the moment. It can be great fun and a huge rush to show off what is "happening right now" to thousands of folks at once. Yes, there's a little ego food there, a bit of a power trip.

Live shots also make sense when you are going too far in the field to get back and get your story on the air. It requires a truck at the scene, and there you are. You might as well be live, not just feeding tape. Let's face it, as much as we rail against them, live trucks are tools of our trade. And they will be used every day. I'm fine with that and expect I'll be live.

The trouble with live shots is, too often they get in the way of telling a better story. They take time to get to, set up, figure out what you are going to do and say. This can really be a drag.

Reporters and photographers get tired of live shots when producers don't care if a live shot helps (or hurts) a story. Last week they wanted me on the roof , thirty stories up, to present a story on tuna tainted with mercury pulled off store shelves. The rationale was that we could see the river from there. Never mind tuna live in the ocean. Why not "live" from the grocery store? All the live trucks were busy, and I wouldn't have had time to get there. In the end I got out of that one, with a reasoned argument, but the E. P. told me only half joking, "OK, but you owe me one." I should have told her I'd pay her back when tuna swim in rivers. All my snappiest comebacks are two hours late.

Be ready and willing to go live. But also be strong enough to stand up against them if they impede a story, or the live shot doesn't make any sense. You can't play that card every day. Smart managers let you throw it out when it's necessary or makes common sense.

## Creature Comforts

Live shots force you to stand out in the elements in all kinds of conditions: darkness and rain, smoke and snow, freezing and hot. Always have a bag at the station packed with the gear you'll need to be comfortable and professional-looking all twelve months. A flashlight and a pack of matches is a good idea, too. Local TV news is not "Survivor", but it is smart to prepare for weather conditions that prevail in your area.

This past year I got soaked because I didn't have my rain pants on board. It had been mostly sunny. An errant thundercloud came along and let loose while we covered a standoff—then live at noon. My fresh-pressed slacks were soaked to the skin in minutes. I was not loving the sensation. It's no fun being stuck out there standing in soggy wingtips. I was not a boy scout, but I like their motto. When you're prepared for the elements, you'll feel better and look better too, when it's time to make live TV.

## Don't Call Me, TV Boy

Most people could not care less about the media. A small minority adore and glamorize us. But some people actually hate the media. It's the ones who hate us you need to watch out for. I have been spit on, laughed at and cursed. Fortunately, never punched in the face. But it does sometimes happen.

Avoid any conflict that could get you hurt. It is not worth it. You can stand up for yourself in a safe and reasonable way. If someone wants to give you a hard time, often the best response is to say something clever and off-putting. That can sometimes de-fuse the situation and they will usually move on and leave you alone. If not, call 9-1-1.

That's what we did when golf balls started hitting the live truck at 5:30 a.m. We were doing the morning live shot in a notoriously media-angry part of the city when the first one bounced off the windshield. I was startled. I called to my photographer, Ole Olson, who was in the back after the second one hit. Then I opened the door and hollered, "Hey what the hell are you doing?" In return I heard, "F*** you, TV Boy". At that point, Ole opened the side door and walked toward a pair of drunken trouble-makers. It scared the hell out of me. I was seriously concerned one of these guys might pull out a knife or gun and kill Ole. That's when I called 9-1-1.

As it turned out, since Ole is six foot three, he was intimidating enough to bring those idiots back to non-violence. But the verbal jousting went on. The pair eventually stumbled off before police arrived.

People can be so rude. Usually, their anger over "corporate media" is unfairly aimed at individuals just trying to do a job. We bit back a little that morning, and it could have turned out worse. Now, it's a reminder to me that angry people are better left alone or, at least handled with care, to be safe.

## Journalists as Terrorism Targets

Remember the Anthrax Killer's letter addressed to "Tom Brokaw"? One might argue the man who sent the letter containing powdered anthrax spores was more a kook than terrorist. In either case, it demonstrates that we in the media are in the cross hairs of domestic terrorists.

News crews might also be targets for terrorists wishing to spread their message. Inside our borders, field news crews need to be aware of people posing as journalists to get access to the press pen. These interlopers may wish to subvert the efforts of journalists there. It doesn't happen often, but seems to be happening more frequently. These people rarely possess credentials and passes necessary for access. They may have talked their way in, to anonymously blend with the corps of journalists for access to an event they wish to disrupt, like a recent Hilary Clinton event before the 2008 election.

We should always be aware and vigilant about people posing as journalists to gain access. They may be dangerous.

Local TV news crews and the media organizations we represent are targets, too. Watch your back at events that might attract protesters and media haters. Pay particular attention before live shots. Watch the backs of colleagues. When one organization gets disrupted, it damages us all.

## It's Not Easy Seeming Insensitive

Reporting live on the sidewalk outside Yamhill county courthouse, I described a defendant who pled guilty to shooting an associate in the head then burying him. I said,

"You'll recall Smith's body was found last month, stuffed in a barrel at a pig farm outside McMinnville".

At that moment, a little old lady who looked half my height and using a cane ambled up behind me. She paused and stared at me.

I could feel her presence, more than see her. Combined with the gruesome words I was saying, it was a surreal, awkward sensation. I actually reacted by laughing. Just one short, breathless chuckle which, when I thought about it, was hard to explain. But I knew and I felt bad. . . for a moment. Then I remembered, this is an odd business. We talk about homicide and mutilation. Sometimes when we do, little old ladies will stop and listen.

## Stand Ups and Teases

Stand-ups and teases are a necessary evil and frequently an afterthought, but they must be done. I have a little different take on stand-ups and teases. I believe viewers want to get to see the person delivering the story—put a face to the voice. Stand ups can be much more than that, offering a demonstrative way of giving a story detail, or showing part of the story that is difficult to sum up in words.

We have a colleague here in Portland that has a tendency to be a little over the top—a bit of a show horse, as we say. But his on-camera stuff is impressive. One time in a live shot about a mudslide, he took a bottle of water, and poured it out on a spot on the hillside. It all ran off, demonstrating how saturated the soil was. Simple but illustrative, and better than just standing there.

I've stood there plenty of times. But I also have done everything from flying a plane to casting a fishing lure. I've jumped in a lake for a story and skied behind a horse (skijoring.) All this to make a story more interesting and understandable. Plus, it's fun, if you have time to do it right.

As for teases. . . Yes, they are a pain. But find a way to make them interesting with a good show and tell. They are often your best chance to sell your story to people who may be about to change the channel and watch something else. A good tease arouses your curiosity. For example, I might do a tease for a story about storm drain runoff dangers like this. As I walk along the curb and kneel down to a storm drain at the corner I say, "I'm Tim Gordon, there is something running down the drain that is killing an important form of life in the river. Coming up at 6, what it is, and what you can do to stop it." Reach people visually, and keep it simple, with just enough information to get their attention, and hopefully they will stick around.

The pesky little necessities and producer pacifiers that are stand ups and teases must be done. Frequently, no one remembers them until you're loading up your gear to high tail it back to the news room or live truck. This relegates them to an afterthought. And while it's true, they're not as important as story gathering, they will air. Done poorly, a hastily shot stand up can bring a fast-paced package to a skidding stop or, in the case of teases, fail to deliver what the name implies.

Consultants spend hours with reporters working on stand ups and teases. Photographers need to know a few things, too.

The media chum line at a neighborhood shooting in Scapoose, Oregon. That's Tim on the right preparing for a live shot. That day we all did the same story from the exact same location.

Practically speaking, teases rarely require much shooting. A pan or tilt from the talent (always start with your reporter in the frame) to an accident scene is about as complicated as a tease should ever be. Teases should last a sentence or two tops. Too much camera movement is distracting. And since teases frequently run two or three in row, you want them to lead smoothly to what follows. A reporter walking toward you as they tease your story is good. Shooting it from a steady bag on the ground or from a perspective above your reporter is better still.

Stand ups are a different animal than teases though they frequently are lumped together. Stand ups are contained within the story or package. That makes them more important. Ideally, a good stand up leads into the next section of script or out of what came previously. They must have a reason to exist and not merely words that could be scripted and covered with video.

The majority of stand ups show reporters standing in one place and talking the entire time. Perhaps the reporter moves a little, but a few steps toward the camera does not make a good stand up. It should have a straight cut in it somewhere. This will accelerate the pace and keep the stand up from slowing down a package. Excessive camera movement is distracting. Nothing moves better than a crisp edit or two and a sound pop. Done well, a stand up may hasten the flow of a good story.

## My Camera Buddy

Reporters appreciate a photographer who can produce necessary items like head phones, lint brush, comb, notepad and pen. Photographers appreciate reporters who carry the tripod without being asked. Reporters who make an effort to fit in lunch for their crew quickly find themselves accepted professionally and personally.

# Breaking News, Story Types and How to Approach Them

## The Reporter-Photographer Team

Breaking news is what makes this job special. It's an adrenaline rush, being at the scene of sometimes amazing events that play out while you watch (and hopefully record.) And you're getting paid to be there! How many can say they felt the heat of the fire up close? Or saw the tear gas fired through the front window into the house. Few know the relief and excitement standing beside searchers when they announce they found the boy in the woods alive. Despite over-selling the title Breaking News, dedicated news people live for the real deal. How well you handle it determines whether you get called to cover breaking news next time.

## In the Moment of Breaking News

Before all of us in the newsroom go off, let's take a deep breath. Think. And make smart decisions that will hold up through the event. Ask some questions. The answers may save some time by concentrating your efforts and make you look good in the end.

- How big is the breaker? Is it the new lead story?

- Who goes? Who is close? Who is best-suited to cover the story?
- What do you lose by pulling people for the breaker?
- Do we need more crews?
- How about an extra body in the field to field produce/pull cable?

Breaking news is difficult to manage and cover because it can cause confusion in a news room removed from the event. It's immediate, often visual, and in many cases affects people: a big fire, the SWAT team neighborhood shutdown, an unpopular court decision. Viewers want to know right now. That's what local TV news delivers. But it looks bad if it isn't done right. A responsive, organized desk and managers are critical to getting off to a quick start. Smart, efficient field crews are the key to getting there, getting it on first, and getting the story straight. I've seen weak responses screw up breaking news coverage with disorganized direction, inaction and lack of focus. Solid decision-making that sends crews out quickly followed by coordinated efforts in the field and at the station help you win this game.

As a field crew, it's critical to be involved from the initial decision-making on out. You'll be the ones on scene, judging needs, newsworthiness and communicating this information back to the station.

Expect to be live as soon as you arrive and get a shot up. Start making calls on the way to gain information before arrival. Once there, get ready for fast information and news gathering, quick composition and fact dissemination. Get ready to pull some cable and set up a light. And hold your bladder, it may be a while. There can be so much going on, focus is key and K.I.S.S. (We're not talking about face paint and glam boots. See chapter three.) Gather as much as you have time for: video, information and sound. Make mental notes of the best video and communicate what it is. Initially, it's about getting it on the air, and reporting it as correctly as the initial information allows.

# The Difference Between a Good and Average Story

People make a story. If it's a story about a bridge, it's a story about the people the bridge affects: the people building the bridge, the people paying for the bridge, the people living near the bridge, and the people driving across it. Don't ever forget the people in your story. They will drive it.

Story telling can make a minute and a half package sing. It is much more than having a beginning, middle and end. It is telling a human being's personal journey, however small or narrow that journey is. In a who, what, where, why and how sense, story telling is about people, what they are going through, how they are affected by a situation or process. Story telling penetrates how people feel, why they act the way they do, and what motivates them. Weaving the human element into the facts of any story is critical. And with an economy of words—just use the best.

Your writing should read in a conversational voice, easy to comprehend and digest. For news, it's often defined as writing "like you're explaining the story to your mother." Having a talent for good story telling and being able to do it in the general assignment world of news is what separates good reporters from mediocre. Story telling is what we strive to do. It's not always easy given the constraints and pressures of a five o'clock deadline, but it's worth aiming for because even if you miss you've likely elevated the story.

Moments make stories memorable. They are the looks, the juicy sound bites, unexpected action, and turning points in a story. They are events that just happen, naturally, which you are fortunate enough to capture. A protester shouting at passersby, the crowd's collective gasp, cops tackling a suspect. Moments all. Moments don't happen in every story, but they happen more often when you are open to them. Wait for them to happen, facilitate them by not getting in the way, and be brave enough to use them.

## General Assignment

This term applies to stories that will be gathered and air the same day. These are the stories pitched in the morning meeting, plus whatever else sticks to the wall. General assignment stories comprise more than three quarters of show's content and do not include special assignments, national stories the network provides, teases, readers, sports and weather.

The load of general assignment stories at my station usually falls to a group of five or six reporters and as many photographers. This "dirty dozen" provide the majority of content for all the shows on any given week day. That we are fewer than half the total number of reporters and photographers employed here, and just a fraction of all the people in the building whose jobs depend on the quality of our news product, is a confounding imbalance. The number of reporters and photographers working general assignment is constantly shifting depending on vacations, illness, special projects etc. So managers have to change their approach almost daily. It's difficult.

## Sweeps Packages and Series Pieces

A kind of temporary insanity grips news rooms during sweeps. News directors and producers get awfully cranky. There is good reason. Their jobs may hang in the balance of sweeps numbers. So for those weeks and months, buckle up and pay attention.

Sweeps stories are longer format, typically two to four minutes. This length has advantages and disadvantages. If you're a photojournalist who has shot enough good video to cover a package this length, editing it can be a pleasure and gauge of your complete skills.

Talk about this important story first with your reporter then include a producer or the news director. Get input and ideas, so you can develop a plan for how you want the story to look. Would the story benefit from tight close-ups of the objects you're talking about? What about people's faces in close-up, reflecting the way they feel? Maybe you want as much movement as possible to emphasize the action of an event your sweeps story is explaining? Think about how you want your story to look. Then manipulate your b-roll and a-roll to reflect that look.

Longer formats almost without exception benefit from fast pacing. A four minute story that does not move can be excruciating. Ideally, a four minute package should feel like three or fewer. This is accomplished with crisp editing. Avoid hanging on a shot longer than four seconds unless it's dynamic and changing. Use lots of natural sound. This device may slow a story a few seconds here and there, but used creatively, it makes stories feel faster. Subtraction by addition. A well-paced story that slows to breath in places moves better than a breathless track-bite-track sprint to the finish line.

Beginnings and endings are particularly important with sweeps and series pieces. A good opening shot and sequence that draws you in to the story is the first, crucial step to an interesting sweeps package. Talk to your reporter first, before he begins writing. Let him know the most visual sequence to use in the beginning. If that's not the sequence your reporter has in mind, make sure his is compelling, too. Use your best sequence to tell the story off the top. Hopefully, you have several good sequences. Any of which would work well to open with. Then you're flexible and the reporter can probably begin the package however he likes and you'll have good video to back it up. Your closing sequence and shot should leave a visual and sonic impression that resonates emotionally.

It's a rare opportunity these days to get to do a long form story. When the Gods are smiling, we get a day to shoot, and a day to write and edit! It's not like this at every station. Some still value long form, in-depth pieces on issues that matter. And once, in the not too distant past, my newsroom valued this type of journalism.

Several years ago, I did a two-part piece on Iraq war military families. The first was about PTSD (post-traumatic stress disorder) suffered by soldiers and how it affects their families as soldiers adjust to life post-combat. An informative, personal story.

The second part was even better. Featuring two families whose husbands were in combat together in Iraq, the two wives and children here at home shared what it was like to be without their daddies and husbands at Thanksgiving. It was a poignant story of hope and fear, sadness and pride. The intersection of emotions made it interesting. The best part was that the two guys were buddies before and during their tour of duty. The wives grew close, but had different feelings about the war. One felt the Iraq war was not worth her husband risking his life. Her friend felt the war effort was noble and worth the risk. This difference of opinion was a surprise we saved until the end of the story.

Both pieces ran four or five minutes, on the long side, but played well. It was a chance to showcase important issues told through compelling people, without rushing it and with greater depth. I hope we're able to tell those types of stories again some day.

## Feature Stories

Some days you have to fight to do feature stories. They get buried under the less interesting but more "important" stories we have to cover like newspaper stories, whatever the competition is covering, breaking news and commodity stories we can't wean ourselves away from. You have to make your case in the morning meeting, but it's usually worth the effort.

More than any other story type, features are gems that viewers talk about and associate with the reporter and the station where it airs. Sometimes, when the news gods are smiling, they just fall into your lap. Other times, they are disguised as a harder story, like the morning a black bear terrorized a neighborhood.

What fun that was, chasing the people and the people chasing the bear. On one hand, a serious story. Residents were told to stay inside. Schools threatened closing. All the while, a black bear

**Moments make stories memorable. The best moments of all show strong human emotion.**

romped through back yards and city streets. The drama was real. So was the opportunity for a little fun. The juxtaposition of emergency vehicle's flashing lights, officers with guns drawn running after a bear whose only crime was trying to find a place to hide. It was an amusing story with a happy ending.

Nobody hurt. The bear fell asleep after receiving several darts from wildlife officers who hauled him back to the wild for release. This was a story where a feature feel naturally fit.

But it usually doesn't work that way. Most full-fledged features are found, developed and then sold to producers and managers. The first challenge is finding them. Look in the middle of the weekly alternative newspaper, the local free magazine, the odd radio report. Better yet, listen to your friends and family, and strangers on the street. If someone tells you something off-beat that piques your interest, ask questions. There is a support group for moms breast-feeding their children beyond toddler-hood? That barbershop quartet Uncle Bob likes so much is made up entirely of WW II veterans? An agility training course for cats? Really. These were all good stories that fit beautifully with the news of the day.

It's rarely an easy sell to get to tell the story, however. With the ever increasing strain on resources, any break from that grinding pattern of quick turn crime stories will require a lot of convincing. Every newsie knows the feature story is the one viewers laugh about or repeat a line from when they gather in the break room. Remind your managers. Then deliver that "water cooler story". Be creative. Have some fun. Doing it well will earn you praise, and the license to do it again.

## On Your Side

On Your Side news is a slogan and style of news-gathering. It's the smaller market version of a "60 Minutes"-type story. We do it with our own reporters playing the part of Dan Rather and doing things like pushing their way into the cheat's office demanding an explanation. This type of journalism is as effective with local rip-off artists as it is with Dan's busted big shots. But the OYS approach occasionally fails for the same reason as some "60 Minutes" stories. Often the stories get bloated with too much reporter presence when it isn't needed.

If the story solves a problem or answers a question, the reporter may get to the bottom of it in an interview. For this, it's effective to stand behind the reporter in a two shot while they ask a good question, then zoom in or step towards the subject as they bury themselves.

Anyone who watches shows like "60 Minutes" or "Frontline" knows reporters frequently are front and center asking questions and chatting up their subjects. That is when reporter presence jumps up a level to reporter involvement.

Gratuitous stand-ups without moving the story forward put the brakes on stories as they gather momentum. How stale is a full body shot of a reporter standing somewhere imparting some aspect of the story that happened there? But it's difficult to avoid. Reporters want to be committed to a story and demonstrate that commitment. They use the stand-up for that and not out of vanity. Sometimes, there's just no other way to get their face in there.

Reporters who "walk and talk" with a subject while both are miked have found a better way to move the story while showing commitment. If a conventional stand-up is the only choice, find a way to break it up. Put some natural sound in it. Match some action and do it in two parts. Remember, most viewers are interested in people, stories and unvarnished facts. Reporters appearing in stories to say something that could be tracked and covered with illustrative video usually does not serve the end product.

## Award Winners Vs. Also Rans

Stories that win awards have compelling moments. I've spent eight hours editing a five minute story, but when it lacked gripping moments, it did not get noticed. I also shot an entire story in twenty minutes that won. Lady gets stuck on a cliff, is rescued and fights with firefighters. A man drives his car into a river, almost drowns and sees God. These had Moments you couldn't turn away from.

How do you get moments into stories with mundane subjects? Talk about it with the reporter. Where the juice in the story? Who's the fiery one to interview? Is there something unexpected that lends a twist to the story? Is there some off-hand comment that sums things up, makes you laugh or places viewers square in the scene? Every good story has one or some of these. The trick is making room for them in the script.

## Commodity Stories: Making Bullshit Sing

Commodity stories are the unfortunate bread and butter of a news diet. And you will spend plenty of time and energy setting them on the table. They are city council meetings, crosswalk enforcement stories, the business grand opening (thank sales for that one), the mayor proclaiming, christening or chastising this, that or the other. So get used to it. Make the story as interesting as possible. Find a colorful person to build the story around. Anticipate and be rolling for any moment of humor, warmth etc.

I did a story about the effort to get a crosswalk painted at a dangerous unmarked intersection. We put together a creative story with people affected in the area, and showed the perils of trying to cross the street. We took the city on, over why they were dragging their feet doing something about it. And in my live shots, I (carefully) demonstrated the danger by trying to cross the street at the unmarked corner. The live demonstration got rave reviews, and so did the story because it was visual and had good everyday folks in it.

Weather stories can also be commodity stories. We recently had our first three day heat wave of the summer season. After a long cool, wet period, the hot weather whipped the news shops into a frenzy. We were charged with covering "exercising in the heat." We did but we also found a swing band down on a dock at the Willamette River, in tuxedos, playing for a video shoot. We added them in our story ("these folks are exercising their musical talents, on a hot day for a tux"). Look for things like this to make an otherwise mundane commodity story inspired. Nuts and bolts need not be rusty. Galvanize them.

But let's face it: not every commodity story will be inspired. The fact is, when you are a rookie, you'll have the energy but fewer tools in your belt to make the mundane interesting. Veteran reporters and photographers have more tools but less energy and inspiration to make bullshit sing. Find balance. Stretch your skills and try new things as a youngster. Dig deep to care a bit more as a vet. The bread and butter, for better or worse, is what keeps us fed.

John MacKenzie taught social studies in Ross, California through the 1970's and 80's. He had a lot of provocative ideas about the media he imparted to classrooms full of seventh graders oblivious to his wisdom. One lesson was an entire hour defining the term "parity product". He offered a simple definition. Every brand of paper towel on the supermarket shelf is basically the exact same thing. So why did our mothers buy one brand and not another? Accept Mr. MacKenzie's definition for now and let local TV news try it on for size. First off, if you watch all four local news stations at the same time (as many newsroom managers spend the news hour doing), you would see a lot pictures and hear a lot of words occurring simultaneously. The generic nature of news is not its most endearing characteristic. The same stuff on the same shelf at the same time.

Another analogy is the chum line of crews reporting on big stories. A media scrum of live trucks, cameras, reporters, interview subjects, etc. Strung out in a row with the same background behind them, telling the same story. When this is the scene, the story is usually pretty good because something big happened. Still, each story and live shot is almost identical to the other.

The little numbers and color schemes on microphone flags, reporters rain parkas, station graphics, sets and backgrounds are all basically similar, however much we pretend the latest is superior.

## How to Approach Boring, Non-Visual Stories

Newspaper stories are what we in the visual news biz fear most: a story weak on pictures. So what to do? First, recognize the visual and non-visual aspects of your story. Thinking visually will help you figure out what you are dealing with. Also, force producers and bosses in the morning meeting to think visually with you. Ask them straight up, "What are the pictures here?"

It helps to brain-storm with this like-minded group; particularly about stories without interesting pictures. And it forces news directors and assistant N.D.'s to rationalize forcing you to do some weak newspaper story best left where it began. But the weak picture argument rarely prevails in the morning meeting. Nine times out of ten, you will be expected to turn this story and for several shows.

When you must do a visually challenged story, use a little creativity in the field. Accept the challenge to tell the story differently and better than the newspaper account. The best person you can speak with about non-visual stories is the photographer who will shoot and edit the piece. They are creative, visual thinkers experienced at playing the best hand they are dealt. Some ideas are better than others. Look for any interesting detail, angle, or person you can find, and use to your advantage. Look for any sound that can make up the deficit: intriguing natural sound, or a short bite from an colorful, on-topic bystander.

Never manufacture visuals. But if you need to demonstrate something, do it in a visual way. For instance, if you need to show distance traveled, hang the camera out the window (carefully) and get the moving shot. You might also shrink that shot into a graphic that shows the distance by the numbers or whatever graphic best represents it. Can the reporter do a demonstrative standup that makes the story more interesting and fill some time? For instance, if the fight that happened yesterday on the street, walk the street and describe what happened: "The yelling started over here, and then moved down the street this way, with people looking on. Then someone picked up a rock from this yard here, and threw it".

No walk and talk stand-ups. Do it in two or three parts. Stories dominated by static shots need extra video, so you can use more of them and keep them shorter, in editing. Motivated pans, tilts and matched action have even greater value in newspaper stories. The savior of visually challenged stories are *people*. Don't forget the human element. Use interesting people to tell your stories and the stories will be interesting.

## Grip and Grins

Some news stories are staged events. We call them Dog and Pony Shows and they go like this.

"Here is the story we're giving you today. We expect you to report it this way."

These are usually press conferences put together by an organization (police, hospital, state etc.) gathering interested parties. Implicit in the event is the organizer's wish to steer it toward a predetermined message. Most of the time, this is fine because there's no ulterior motive or anything to hide. There's no getting around most dog and pony shows. Just shoot it and move on to the next assignment.

Very infrequently, the dog and pony show is set up to prevent journalists from digging deeper into a story. See the section "Be the Curmudgeon". An example would be a police press conference about some misconduct episode that excludes the officers involved. Or a hospital's press conference arranged to discuss a patient without allowing any questioning of the patient or doctors. In these situations, look for the main decision maker and tell them of whom you wish to ask questions. If they won't allow that, inform the producer and decide if the story is still worth reporting. It's not much of a story if you can't ask questions freely of all interested, involved parties.

## Public Relations and News

Public relations people desire attention from TV news. Every day and particularly on the week end, we get press releases from public relations companies about groups they represent who want TV time. Typically, we try to avoid these staged events, but occasionally succumb in the interest of filling time. Another necessary evil. The relationship between public relations-generated press releases and the news organizations they are courting is uneasy. We, in news, like to think that the only news we cover is real news, hard news, breaking news. But sometimes we have to rely on more predictable events to fill out the edges of a half hour show, let alone two hours on week days.

Some p. r. sponsored events are more interesting and news worthy than others. Anything with a hard news angle will get our attention (i. e. citizens voluntarily turning in fire arms.) Staged events stand a better chance of attracting TV cameras if the story is visual (i. e. dancers in bright costumes on Cinco de Mayo.) Good human interest may arouse some producer's curiosity and a crew or photographer will be sent out (i. e. giving free Thanksgiving baskets to needy families.)

There's got to be a good reason for TV news to bother with a p. r. event. It's not enough for the sponsor to be terrific and the cause unimpeachable. For example, the local branch of United Cerebral Palsy does great work. They sponsor a walk every summer for their members. We rarely go just for the walk, but when they offer a member with an engaging story then we usually find our way down there and present a vosot on the story and walk.

One last piece of advice for public relations people who desire the attention of local TV news: Do not schedule events to happen an hour or two before the news hour. This simply does not give us enough time to shoot, log, write and edit the story in time to make our slot. If the event schedule is soft and you desire media coverage, ten to one o'clock p. m. are convenient hours for journalists with a daily deadline.

## Election Year Revenue and Stories

Election years are historically the time when the advertising cup fills up and spills down the side. It does not leave a stain, however. Generally it results in an increased stock price and smiley faces for investors and portfolio managers. The greatest beneficiaries remain the networks, versus cable. Most political campaigns spend 75 percent of their total advertising budget on television ads. Almost all of that is spent to air "spots" on the networks, national and local. More will be spent on cable channels than ever before, but that will still be less than ten percent of the network's take. About half of what's spent for cable spots will buy popups and adspace on the internet.

It breaks down this way, as of Fall 2012. The upcoming Presidential election and numerous congressional races will generate upwards of 4 billion dollars in advertising revenue for television stations. This is unprecedented. Some forecasters predict 6 billion! In 2008, both parties filled the catwalk with candidates who dished out 2.5 billion dollars. This year's models will strut further, though they are fewer in number. There are just a few gubernatorial races and likely just one Democratic candidate for president, Mr. Obama. Deep pockets there.

The question of how fewer candidates have more money to buy advertising time than four years ago cannot be answered just by inflation or a changed economy. Corporations and unions may contribute to their candidates of choice without a spending limit for the first time in a decade. Expect them to take advantage of this renewed, special freedom.

It would be nice if while all this money is pouring in, some trickled down to local TV newsrooms. That's a tricky equation; budgets are made a year, sometimes years in advance. How election year advertising dollars fit and fill those budgets is difficult to trace. Some of those dollars may be spent on new gear, or new sets and graphics. There is no expectation of financial reward for journalists in local TV news during a profitable election year. That goblet is passed between managers and the sales staff upstairs, if station owners share it at all.

Stories about candidates and their true believers do find their way into the daily rundown during the election cycle. These are generally fun and often insightful stories revolving around important issues, fervent politicos and often the candidates themselves. One may have a glimpse into the personality of important national figures who visit and desire TV time. This is interesting to say the least. Which is not to say that the Hilary Clinton event in Portland was as much of a gas as hanging around backstage before the Bruce Springsteen show. It is work, after all.

## Staged Events

Some staged events are news. One example was the famous war photograph "Raising the Flag on Iwo Jima" by Associated Press photographer Joe Rosenthal. It's the only photograph to win a Pulitzer Prize the same year it was taken. One of the most enduring moments of World War II, it's a symbol of the United States Marine Corps whose members are seen in the photo.

Five day after the invasion of Iwo Jima, the Marines raised a small American flag atop Mt. Suribachi the morning of February 24. Seen by many Marines that day, it was a boost for morale in the midst of a bloody battle that would last over a month on that bomb scarred island. Someone in the top brass recognized the importance of the event and organized another flag-raising the same day with a larger flag and several photographers to capture the image.

So while we try to avoid them, some staged events are news

worthy. It is the journalist's job to find the best story at the event then get access to the people and places that will tell that story.

## Press Conferences

This is an event where it often helps to work with your colleagues at other stations to make the affair run smoothly. Helping set up lights, arranging microphones in a stand, putting the podium or table in a location to take advantage of a background. Reporter/ photographer teams should try to get a little edge during this shared opportunity.

The first order is to make sure your sound from the podium is clean and loud. Hard wiring from the podium microphone straight to the camera is common. It eliminates problems associated with wireless microphones, like interference from the other mikes, weak batteries or intrusive radio frequency.

Many press conferences are staged events. Someone might read a statement. Often the source is a member of the family or an

**A decent cutaway of news soldier, Bob Heye. Talk to the tie.**

official. Part of the ground rules might disallow direct questions from the media. This may be a red flag. If you can't ask questions directly, you may not want to participate. This is not a last minute decision, but rather something to discuss with a producer as soon as it comes to your attention. A phone call should go out to who-ever is organizing the press conference. Will direct questions be allowed? Often, all that's being offered is a statement and no questions after.

If you arrive at the event to find they won't allow questions from the media, you can't do much. If it's a family who want to share a picture and recollection of the deceased but have no involvement in how he died, a statement may be sufficient. If the person speaking has more information than they are offering or is contained in their statement, then the media has every right to ask for elaboration or clarification. If questions are still not allowed, this is a red flag.

If subjects are willing, take the opportunity to speak with them away from the podium. Their answers are often more spontaneous and interesting than what may be offered above the microphone cluster. Look for ways to improve the lighting wherever the subject stands during the press conference. A key light at minimum will do. Two key lights with one slightly less bright (or directed slightly away from the podium) is best. Position your camera on the side less bright.

Think ahead to editing the story. The first matched action sequence you can gather is the wide shot of the person stepping to the microphone

then cutting to whatever bite the reporter has chosen. Shoot this wide shot for every speaker as they approach the microphone, anticipating your reporter will select a bite from them. That way, you have one matched action sequence for every speaker.

Know when to break off sticks and begin gathering cutaways and b-roll of the event. Work it out ahead of time with the reporter that she'll let you know when she has ample sound. Having plenty of good cutaways comes in handy with stories that may wind up relying on them.

## Thumb Suckers

Some stories are so short and straightforward, a child could present them. These are often commodity stories, like gas prices or a busted meth lab. Doing them live from the gas station or beside the goggled, hazmat suited clean-up crew requires little more than a emphatic retelling of the facts. Easy stuff. Just remember to remove your thumb from your mouth before the live shot.

## When Is a Plane Crash Not Breaking News?

The plane crash referred to in the title is an analogy for any hot sounding scanner traffic over which the newsroom gets its collective thong in a knot, not realizing that the breaking news event they're salivating over is no longer dynamic. If the plane has crashed and authorities are just maintaining a line until the Federal Aviation Administration arrives, then the story is not breaking or changing much. When the fire department is still on scene putting out a fire or rescuing a passenger, the story is breaking and you should get there as quickly as possible.

There are exceptions to the knee jerk reaction. Some yield results that leave your colleagues wondering why they didn't think of it first. Occasionally in these situations, when most of the competition is standing around waiting for the FAA, you might get the jump on them by finding some personal angle or some interesting information no one has bothered to research.

Recently, a light plane taking off from Hillsboro Airport radioed to the tower it was having engine trouble. An air traffic controller recommended the pilot make an emergency landing at tiny Oak Grove Airport a few miles away. Unfortunately, the pilot was unable to land safely and crashed. He died at the scene. All this was known by the desk when we were moved from our original story assignment located half an hour away.

We knew after a few phone calls that the effort was strictly to recover the pilot. No one would move the plane until the Federal Aviation Administration arrived to gather evidence for the latter. They investigate every fatal crash involving aircraft. This being the case, the reporter and I decided to stop by the Oak Grove Airport to see if we could find out anything else. The airport manager was forthcoming and told us weather conditions were crucial to the plane's landing difficulty. He shared several other details that went into the script and some personal information about the pilot with whom he was acquainted.

When we arrived at the crash, last but not least, we'd gathered considerably more information than the competition. They were waiting for a police P. I. O. who knew next to nothing. We gathered video from that scene and put together a more informative, personal and memorable story than the competition that day. It was accomplished because we made our story about a person inside an event rather than the event with a person's name attached to it.

## What's the Mayor Good For?

*Sound.* The mayor turns up regularly at staged events. It's not a coincidence when the mayor happens to be helping paint the school on Saturday. That's why you're there. Run a few good questions by her. There may be something else your producer wants the mayor to comment on besides freshly, painted walls. It's all fair game.

*An important looking show.* Producers love mayor sound and her picture because it makes their shows look important. If you have mayor sound, inform the producer. That sound will usually find a home in one show or another. Often it's the cold open or tease video.

## Night Siders Cover Meetings

Meetings are considered a bit of a curse by night siders who cover them regularly. After working many night shifts the last ten years, I feel qualified to offer a photojournalistic approach to this common story setting. By "meetings" we mean any group where people address an audience that's seated, including assemblies, church etc. These ingredients are not a recipe for excitement and rarely does the final product generate much interest outside the attendees. But the topics and individuals steering the discussion are very much the stuff of good local news. And the first rule of covering a meeting for TV news is people. All good stories have human beings at the heart of the story and so it should be with stories gathered at a meeting. That said, no meeting should wind up on TV unless something important is decided, someone important will be speaking or there's the expectation of contention and argument.

An important city council or school board meeting is the type of story that belongs on the local TV news. Even if that meeting is more of a newspaper story.

NIGHTSHIFT LAND

Well, as you can see behind me this breaking news is spectacular!

Just incredible!

I'll step out of the way now...

and let the pictures tell the story...

It's also true that too many meetings wind up on the 11 o'clock news, usually for lack of any new or better stories. A fair measure for whether a meeting deserves to be covered lies in the answer to this question.

"Would I be interested in attending this meeting myself?"

Take off the producer's hat for a minute and put on what most viewers are wearing at eleven. Jammies. If you would not be interested in attending a meeting about budget adjustments or teacher work days or a city council hearing for citizen input on the proposed sidewalk improvements, then don't expect anyone at home lying in bed to stick around for more than five seconds. The sound of already tired viewers grabbing for their remotes at 11:11 p. m. does not have to be audible to be perceived. Put a person at the center of the story; use them as a vehicle to describe the meeting. You might have to interview them at home or work, before the meeting. This requires planning, but in the end enhances your story and keeps viewers interested.

Meetings can make for pretty good news stories provided there's some contention. The best stories have people at the center and balanced presentation of the issue dividing them. Certain visuals put these stories over better than others. A "back and forth" shot for action/reaction editing can really move a package along. Keep the two sides framed on opposite sides in interviews, so butted together they appear to talk at each other. If you've gathered some good moments panning from one to the other as they're arguing, consider standing back and shooting the most animated person from behind the least vocal while still keeping the latter soft focused in the foreground. The more worked up people get, the more they talk with their hands. When someone does, focus on it and stay there for awhile. Compelling sound bites with something other than faces in the frame break up the monotony of talking heads.

Clear, loud audio from the meeting is critical to how your story goes over at eleven. Getting it can be a challenge. It works well to have a reporter hold a remote microphone and position themselves

to gather sound. If there's a speaker amplifying sound to the audience then you can put a microphone in front of it or hang the lavaliere mike in front of it. If the city or school provides multiple audio feeds you can plug into, that's best. If you don't have a reporter, speaker or mult box to gather sound, then you have to get as close to your subjects as possible with a stick microphone. My Sennheiser on a curly cord is perfect. It's usually a little uncomfortable at first. Participants act a little nervous initially, but they get used to the camera, microphone and photojournalist in their face. It's just the way it works. Standing as near your subject as you can is a rule of good photography.

Don't keep your camera above the heads of an audience the entire time. Position your camera and sticks to get an audience's-eye view. When you're sitting in an assembly or church, you see and hear a speaker between the heads of people in front of you. The reversal looks good, too. Stand behind the speaker, shooting back at an attentive audience member (with the speaker in foreground, soft-focused.) I don't know how many meeting stories I've seen with every shot above the audience's head. Meetings are boring enough. Get perspectives that make you feel like you are there. Look for any small details that help tell the story and shoot them tightly. These close-ups will fit nicely in editing. End your story with as much emotion as possible and you may temporarily defeat the meeting curse.

## How to Persuade or Opine in a News Story

Do not pontificate in your script. If you believe the girl was beaten unfairly by the cop, let her brother say it or a bystander. That gets the story across without editorializing or subjectivity. Remember, most viewers don't care what your opinion is. They want an objective re-telling of what is known with relevant sound bites and compelling pictures.

It's possible you may not be able to gather the sound appropriate for the story you are telling. When that happens, reporters may feel the need to inject the appropriate, even necessary, emotion in their script and track. That is not the best route to travel, however. Here's an alternative.

A fourteen year old boy was hanging out at a Burger King in Longview, Washington with his thirteen year old girl friend. He is white. She's mixed race. After leaving the establishment in broad daylight, they were assaulted. The boy's jaw broken and the girl choked by an eighteen year old white supremacist. Motorists drove by, but none stopped to help.

A few days later, we went to interview the boy's mother. She told us at the outset, she was nervous. Nobody wants to make white supremacists angry at them. Like snitching on a Crip in East L. A., speaking out against neo-Nazis can be dangerous. So she was guarded in her descriptions of the incident and her son's condition. She described the racially motivated beating of two adolescents by an adult as the teens being "picked on". In fact, she used the term numerous times during the interview. It was frustrating trying to get at how she felt, but she would not open up.

We had a story that needed emotion and accurate description. Two kids getting beaten badly by an adult because one was white and the other non-white is worse than being "picked on" and ought to stir a little outrage. Unfortunately, the mom could not provide it. Knowing we weren't going to inject it into the script with track that would have tilted the story subjectively, we had to go elsewhere for it. In this case, we found it at the diner around the corner. Between bites of Sunday breakfast, these Longview residents gave us plenty of emotion, analysis and explanation of how it could happen. They provided the emotion and conscience an assault victim's mother was too afraid to express. And kept our opinions out of it.

## The Hand Shake

If you've ever heard the expression "it could be worse", you know it usually holds true for whatever lousy circumstance you're describing. There is one geographical exception to this rule which occurs whenever you are unfortunate enough to be in Longview, Washington. Economically depressed since the Clinton administration and the end of big timber contracts, the town is stumbling to get back on its feet.

On a drizzly day (Are there any other here?), my reporter, Joe English and I were trying to run down a councilman and the city attorney to comment on a white power group's application for a permit to hold a rally in town. We also wanted to contact any member of that group, though that was in doubt from the start. White supremacists are supremely shy of the press as a rule.

A city councilman told us off the record that the group's permit request was in possession of the city attorney who wanted to deal with all media questions herself. She was conveniently gone that

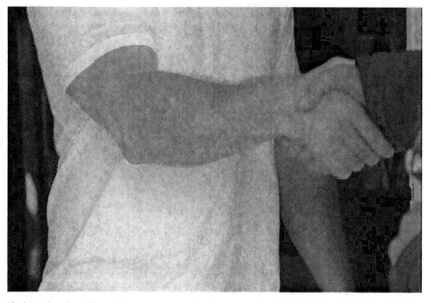

**Shaking hands with a white supremacist is always preferable to getting beaten up by one. But you might not want to air it in your story.**

Friday, however. And by the way, we were told, the white supremacist's phone number on the application went to a disconnected number.

After gathering b-roll of the rally location, we interviewed two councilman. The second one produced a copy of the permit request. We were thrilled to see beside the name and disconnected phone number, a street address. Cutting it close to our deadline, we drove immediately to a tidy house at the edge of Longview. Joe knocked and we found our white power organizer at home and in a fairer mood than most we've met from his gang/group. He spoke in sound bites. Grammar good. Extremely clean cut, naturally. Really, it was a pinnacle experience with a white supremacist. They're typically a pretty prickly bunch, but not this guy. He spoke, we rolled and finally we all shook hands and left.

Joe called back to the news room to tell them our story had changed. We'd interviewed a member of the white power group and had good sound. Producers seemed pleased. We drove straight to the rally location to do our live shots.

Once there we had about thirty minutes to cut the package and feed it. The satellite window was for 5:10 to 5:20. We had a few problems with the laptop and had to power down twice. The window came. I laid in the last shot of the hand shake good bye. Joe, myself and our engineer all looked at it and declared it good. We fed and immediately ran outside to do our live shot, which came off nicely. Joe remarked casually we should "keep our jobs another day."

When I got back to the news room, the N. D. was waiting for me. "Can you come in to my office?"

Seven words you don't want to hear. It's never good. I could feel the last shot of the package rumbling around in my stomach.

"What can you tell me about the last shot of that package?"

Those open ended questions are the worst. Well, I told him, we thought the hand shake demonstrated objectivity on our part. Joe and I had said as much on the drive home. Of course, in the interest of full disclosure, Joe's wife called five minutes later asking him why he'd shaken the white supremacist's hand.

To be honest the objectivity argument sounded better in the car than in his office. The N.D. thought the hand shake implied acceptance and agreement on our part. He reminded me of something I've heard before—that pictures carry as much weight as any words or sound bite.

# Work Smart

## Be a Field Producer

Don't limit yourself to being a photographer or reporter in the field trying to shape your story. Think of yourself as a Field Producer taking responsibility for every aspect of news gathering. Considering the entire story rather than your specific duties is liberating and empowering.

This field producer approach fits the collaborative effort idea promoted throughout this book. As a reporter, develop an eye for visual composition. As a photographer, develop an ear for good sound bites and a mind for factual content. As a team, share your insights with each other to tell the best story possible.

## Slow Down and Breath

We have a tendency to get excited in breaking news situations. That's natural. When you're live, use some of that energy to convey the immediacy of the situation. But don't let your excitement flood out and overpower your reporting. You may blurt out everything all at once with little inflection or race ahead of viewers who can't keep up. You may forget to mention something important or use language that tells the story inaccurately.

No matter what your deadline is, it's better to slow down and

**When shooting interviews wide, make sure there's something to look at in every part of the frame around the subject.**

listen. The other day, we covered a fairly sensational story of a man who allegedly hired a co-worker to kill his estranged wife. The wife strangled the would-be killer in her own home, as he attempted to beat her to death with a hammer. The husband was jailed. When the wife finally decided to speak with the media, it was with me alone with my cameraman. An important and exclusive story. When we spoke, she was an articulate and thoughtful woman, who cared very much about her family. Her husband included. In the context of the interview, I mistook her to say that she loves her husband, at least in a caring way. What she actually said was she loved her husband (past tense), and in fact continued on to say "things are different now". In my haste, I reported she still loved her husband (present tense).

The story aired and she was not happy. In fact, she was angry. I felt terrible, as my intention was (and always is) to present a person's feelings as accurately as possible. We made changes to every story that followed, and I spoke at length with her about misrepresenting her feelings for her ex.

Undue haste may result in sloppy journalism. That was the root of my mis-reporting, hurrying and feeling hurried while logging the interview. In the end she understood and forgave. If I had slowed down and listened to the tape a second time, I would have heard her correctly and reported the story accurately. This was a dozen years into my career, proving that even the most experienced among us have opportunities to learn, especially from our mistakes.

Take a breath. Pauses allow viewers to follow along. They allow you to get some oxygen to your brain, assess as you report, get from one place to the next. And you won't feel like you just ran a marathon after the producer gives you the all clear.

## Cozy Up to Your Subject

To get interview subjects to wear a wireless microphone, sometimes takes a little finesse. They may be reluctant, while you need their sound for the story. In these situations be nice, not pushy. I've seen a few reporters get bossy and it has always backfired. Once you set the lav mike clipped on and transmitting, the goal should be allowing the interview subject to relax enough to give thoughtful answers.

If you're doing the interview without a reporter, keep it conversational and relaxed. Avoid formality. Standing behind the camera, asking questions one after another is a recipe for nervous answers. Light the interview and seat the subject. Lock down your camera then sit down with your subject and have the type of conversation you would with a family member. Informal, friendly, honest. Know the story going in and try to illicit responses that tell that story. If you run out of questions before enough sound has been gathered, consider the most important who, what, why, when, where and how's of the story as you understand it. Don't be afraid to follow up on answers that might sound contrary to the story. These details give a fuller picture and may give the story greater precision.

Keep a keen ear out for emphatic, easy-to-understand sound bites that last five to fifteen seconds. These will best fit a minute and a half package or vosot.

With reporter interviews, save questions until after the reporter is finished or you are brought into the conversation. Photographers that pepper interview subjects between the reporter's queries interrupt the relationship reporters create before asking a big question. It can turn an interview into an interrogation, which makes people defensive.

Yes, please don't interrupt me during my interview of the subject. Photographer communication at this point should be with the reporter, a look or sign that signifies changing a shot between questions, etc. It is appropriate when the interview is finished to invite the photographer to ask any questions they might have.

## Be the Wind Shield

The most difficult events we cover involve tragedy of some kind. When people die in an untimely or unnatural way, it is frequently news. Unfortunately in situations where family is involved, there is rarely any happy ending.

One of the ugliest of these stories unfolded on the Oregon coast. A family man named Christian Longo murdered, mutilated and then buried his wife and three children in suitcases in the waters around Newport Bay. This cowardly act stood in dark relief to the two post card pretty locations he chose to dispose of the bodies. How anyone could commit an act like that in this beautiful place remains incomprehensible. Within a day, news crews from Seattle, Portland, CNN and all the networks arrived. They created a lot of excitement and what some thought negative publicity for a quiet town hibernating between tourist seasons.

Later described by doctors as a narcissist and sociopath, Longo was apprehended in Mexico, sharing a cabana with a German tourist and passing himself off as a writer for the New York Times (the subject of a book.) It all generated massive public interest.

Usually, the only decent news that comes out of really awful stories like this is some small consolation for the family that's left. A body is recovered, so the family can bury their loved one and get some closure and hopefully move on. Or the perpetrator is brought to justice, removed from society and punished. Neither is a happy ending when you lose a sister, brother, father or mother. There is no silver lining for the family.

Fifteen months after he killed his wife and kids, a jury decided Christian Longo should die by lethal injection. Residents of Oregon and people around the world were keen to know the thoughts of the eight women and four men who found him guilty. There was a lot of scrambling for interviews with them. Word got out that a competitor, Channel Eight, lined up one jury member and was meeting them inside the court house that afternoon. Our reporter, Bob Heye, heard this, waited <u>outside</u> the court house for over an hour until the jury member arrived to be interviewed upstairs. Bob engaged him with cameras rolling, got the interview and beat the competition. In securing this story, Bob played out one of his favorite adages.

"Some days you're the wind shield. Some days you're the bug."

—BOB HEYE

## Under Promise, Over Deliver

The subtitle above is a good one to consider before you get the phone call.

"How's your story coming along?"

There's a tendency to exaggerate how well your story is going, in morning meetings, phone conferences on the road, etc. Every reporter and photographer wants their story to be the lead, so we speak optimistically to entice producers to perhaps move up a story in the show. Big mistake.

Don't let excitement get the best of you when informing producers how your story is going. Giving the news room unrealistic expectations about a story you can't quite deliver doesn't help anybody. Being realistic about how the story is going while working to deliver the best pictures and sound will seldom disappoint. Of course, if you've got something terrific, be it pictures, emotion or just a great story, let everyone know immediately, so they can tease it and get prepared.

# In the Cage of the Beast

## News Room Politics

Politics play out in most offices, but newsroom politics are notorious for a reason. It's a combustible combination of creative, inquiring minds, big egos, deadline pressures, business realities and under-talented managers who enjoy playing with matches. Tension and disgruntled minions exist in every newsroom. Many would say "nowhere worse than mine". But I think I'm the loser in this category. Three station sales in 6 years, layoffs, losing benefits, poor management, sliding ratings, hiring cheap replacements, loss of vision, bad producers, new automated production systems taking jobs and making newscasts inflexible and ugly to watch. I can only hope it gets better, because I love what I do. In the meantime I fight for better conditions while staying out of the unproductive political fray, and do the best job I can despite the circumstances. I am not alone.

It's more difficult to be the boss than to criticize her. And I have had some good bosses. I have a pretty good one now. But in thirteen years, my experience is uneven. Only three out of fifteen news room managers I've worked with possess the golden combination of solid news judgment <u>and</u> some people skills.

How does one survive, navigate and thrive in a work environment like this? It would be nice to say a solid work ethic and high journalistic standards trump politics. It can. But many good men have gone down in flames despite working hard and doing good work.

The best advice I can give to any student or small market careerist is several fold. Love to shoot, report, edit or write good TV news stories. Persevere to that end and don't be afraid to lobby hard to make the stories you work on better. Don't play any more politics than you must to survive. Look out for like-minded brothers and sisters. You'll need each other.

## The Morning Meeting

Most newsrooms start the day with a morning meeting where everyone brings their coffee and sits together to plan the day. A necessary evil, and a sometimes painful process. The pressure to contribute solid story ideas can make or break you. It's difficult to come up with original, interesting ideas every day. And discouraging when you are assigned the daily grind stuff despite your effort and ideas.

Let's consider the half full cup of joe. The morning meeting is an important start to the news gathering day—a meeting of minds where intelligent people discuss current events and ideas then come up with a game plan for the day. It is your chance to speak your mind, share your story ideas, and suggest doing something better than what has been developed by the assignment desk. Embrace the opportunity to shape daily news coverage.

The morning meeting varies from newsroom to newsroom, so there is hope your experiences will be positive. There are ways to prepare. First, if you have a special area of interest, develop a " beat". You will meet people who feed you ideas. You will do stories that will lead to other stories. Your own interest in the area will spark ideas. Next, part of your job as a reporter and photographer is to read a newspaper, get online, listen to the radio, and basically be up on current events, locally, nationally, and globally. Being informed will keep your brain active, geared to the news cycle, and help you generate new ideas to pitch in the meeting.

The days will be long. Getting up early to read the paper or get on your computer isn't much fun. But it can make your day a lot easier by avoiding the anxiety that comes with having nothing to contribute at the table. Ideas will come to you as you drive along, see something, talk on the phone, or are at home with your family. Create a list, and you'll never be without a story to pitch when it's your turn at the table.

## Treating the Symptom

Many things in life may be seen more clearly through the lens of fishing. Even the current state of local TV news. When someone pays you to take them fishing (and catch fish), there is strong motivation to deliver. Money, reputation and, potentially, a returning client are all on the line. You get that client into fish by increasing his odds for success: casting into the most productive runs at the right time of the evening with a fly that fooled fish yesterday. Finally, you put that lure where trout are holding that moment. Taken together you have a recipe for fish catching and, most important, a happy fisherman who had his moment and photograph to show around the office. A good guide does everything possible to improve the chances for this outcome.

So it is in the news game. Right from the start, in the morning meeting, reporter's and photographer's story ideas are given a fair listen. The best story ideas will find a place in the news that day. These are the stories they'll work hardest on and do well because they have a personal attachment. The other advantage to letting field crews do stories they have enterprised is that story will likely only appear on your news. Originality and differentiation in a newscast is a big plus.

Crews with a big story leave as early as possible, so they may be able to get themselves into position to gather that great moment or interview. Also, an early start gives crews a better opportunity at the end of the day to put some additional polish on the writing and editing. Finally, crews out in the field are busy concentrating on writing, editing and putting those finishing touches on their story. Newsrooms concerned with successful outcomes take care to not interrupt them any more than is necessary.

Were success in story telling, originality and good coverage the goal of TV newsrooms, the previous description might be the norm instead of exceptional. Rather, reporters are handed story ideas producers want for their shows. These are usually researched straight from the newspaper that day and exactly like producers at competing stations are handing their reporters at that moment. Not much originality there. And it's rarely a story into which the reporter and photographer are likely to put their story telling soul. Professionals put as much soul into it as they can.

Typically, morning meetings last too long. Crews with lead stories for five or even four o'clock frequently don't leave the newsroom until after eleven with a long drive ahead of them. This leaves barely enough time to gather the simplest elements. Little thought may be given to a story's potential and what elements would make it most interesting. This makes complete, balanced coverage difficult. Even the relatively obvious benefit of not bothering field crews with trivial phone calls and interruptions is seldom recognized. Producers and assignment desk managers sitting across from each other call reporters asking the exact same question and with a deadline looming.

So it is under the last set of circumstances, we work as diligently, creatively and professionally as we can. And when a reporter gets sloppy, they are punished. It is always easier to treat symptoms rather than the root cause.

## The Stressful Job of Producing

Producers have a brutal job. Maybe that's what makes them so needy. Here's the thing: there are some very good producers.

I love a good producer, one that really knows how to write, put together a show and then run the newscast flawlessly from the booth. A good producer manages multiple tasks as the show runs, but is still able to make you feel like your shot is the top piece of business. They give time warnings and cues. That's a skill set.

The problem is too few producers embody that skill set. In fact, there just aren't enough producers, let alone good ones. I don't know why. Maybe they want to be in front of the camera. Producing doesn't pay as well as it used to. Producers are paid slightly less than photojournalists, though some earn more. It's become increasingly the case that any warm body will do. So producers come in with very little experience; that's all the station can entice for what they're paying.

Add to that the fact that many stations are "producer driven". This means producers have too much power over the content of news programming and the people who gather it. This power is often given them by a News Director or assistant N. D. who formerly produced. That's the way it is in half the news rooms I've worked in. Then the youngest, least experienced people in the news room determine which are the most important stories of the day.

Producers are a valuable part of the team and should be treated as such. Maybe if that opinion prevailed, it would become a job to which more talented people might aspire. Then we could expect the cream of the crop, instead of just anybody. If you have aspirations to produce, I hope you're good and I hope you go for it. And I hope you'll be a reasonable collaborator and not just needy.

For reporters and photographers in the field, producers can be like grains of sand in the Coppertone of news gathering. But producers are insatiable. They need to fill a show. They need it to come off without a hitch. They need to get it done! They may have a news director or executive producer breathing down their neck. This creates a must-have mentality. The rub occurs when the producer's expectations differ from the story crews are gathering or actually find when they get out in the field.

It figures a reporter and photographer would have a lot to say about producers. We should give it a whole chapter titled "Our Rant on Producers" or "How I Lost Two Hours of Sleep Every Night for a Year". It's easy to be hard on producers but running down the checklist of things that need fixing in dysfunctional newsrooms, producers are more a symptom than the actual problem.

If your car is running rough and stinky, black smoke pours out the tailpipe, the problem probably isn't the tailpipe. In order to fix a complex system running poorly, start at the top and work your way down. And so it is with news. CEO's trim the budget and

staff of stations they own to please stockholders. General managers and news directors rarely bite the hand that feeds them, so they pass along the diminution of news to everyone in the news room, including producers. Producers who disagree with news directors get frustrated and quit. Most go along to get along and pass down whatever's handed to them. Producers aren't solely responsible for the cheapening of local TV news. They're just the tailpipe. The managers and executives who drive producers and think a lean news room staff and budget is the best way to produce local TV news are causing the stink and need replacing.

It hurts me to say anything bad about producers. Most are good people: smart, funny and hard working. But in the interest of truth and trying to get this beast to behave, you can't leave out producers.

Frequently, producers need stories put together sooner than reporters and photographers are able to do it. In these circumstances, it's critical to keep producers abreast of stories that aren't going to make "slot". Before that, you and your reporter should make every effort to turn the thing in a jiffy. Just crash it together, as we say. If circumstances prevent a quick turn, it's imperative crews notify the producer ten or fifteen minutes ahead of the show. If you need to have a story "floated" more than once a year for anything other than technical problems, it's not the producer's fault. Avoid last minute fire calls.

If stories don't come in on time, shows may start off with a limp or turn into a train wreck. Then producers are cursing us in the field, perhaps justifiably. As reporters and photographers need to look out for other, so too do crews in the field need to consider producers.

Producers have a difficult job. They rarely get the same pat on the back as reporters when a story works. Most photographers and reporters admit they could never be producers because producers only leave the building for lunch. But they get lunch! They also may have the news director peering over their shoulder. Producers seem to log more hours in the news director's office, which isn't fun either.

There's a story about a news director once remarking he favored a producer because he knew that producer would "eat glass" if he asked him to. The comment was probably intended as a joke, but there's a at least a shard of truth to it. Some producers will do just about anything to please their boss.

A well produced show can have some seemingly unpredictable twists and turns. These usually come in the form of live shots where something is actually happening. This may require a producer to deviate from their rundown a little and perhaps go to the live shot a little early or return to a live shot when the action starts happening. That's good television, but more difficult than ever to carry off because of unwieldy software that forces every change in the rundown to be keyed in ahead of time. With a dynamic live element, a well produced show can be informative, hold your interest and whet your appetite for stories upcoming. A little humor is nice too.

Field crews appreciate producers who don't try to determine what a story is from their desk or at the morning meeting. Experienced producers consider what reporters and photographers have to say about stories they are trying to own. When producers aren't afraid to be a little flexible, news gathering and live TV become the dual pleasures they should be. The give and take between field crews and producers is as complicated and critical to a quality news product as the reporter/photojournalist relationship.

Producers have the advantage of seeing the entire day's news. Reporters and photographers concentrate on their story and are often unaware of any other. Producers are people with a general curiosity. They're fundamentally good writers, pretty savvy with technology and know to chew glass into little bits before they swallow.

## The News Director

They come along every few years—a vagabond group. You never know what you'll get or how road-weary they will be. News Directors have responsibility over the entire operation, including news content, personnel and budget. Some news directors are good, but some are not. Be ready for changes when they arrive. They must make their mark.

Some N. D.s will be decent teachers. A few will have leadership and people skills to inspire the news team. But if that's not the case at your shop, it's best to keep to your work. Do it the best you can. Grow your own career. If you run around trying to please everyone at once, you'll go crazy. Do your job with energy and passion.

I've worked under ten N. D.s at five stations in twelve years. Three have been solid—the others have not.

One of my former N. D.s is currently facing criminal charges for, among other things, abandoning a wife and children to avoid child support, changing his name and using a fake social security number, stealing money from his invalid mother (let me take a breath here), as well as harboring, together with his girlfriend, a young "sex slave" in their household! All this over a number of years where he continued to work in television news and actually wrote books about television news! Enquiring minds need only google "portland news director sadomasochist" for the full wiki scoop.

One of the best News Directors I've worked for is hands-on, effective, professional and friendly. She asked for input from the beginning from the newsroom crew and developed a plan for how we'd operate. She offered criticism and compliments. She even inspired me to care more about what I was doing. It had been a while, and there was a jaded crust on me that was pretty thick. I've always worked hard and thought I'd done good work, but it was rare to have a manager communicate with me about it, offering compliments and suggestions to improve. She proofed and approved sweeps stories, and other daily turns as well. This hands-on professionalism is unusual in my experience for local TV news directors, unfortunately.

## Anchors

Nearly everyone else in the newsroom gives news anchors a pretty hard time behind their backs. It goes with the territory.

Many see anchors as overpaid, over-opinionated dinosaurs that don't work too hard. Some of it is fact, some jealousy. News anchors earn their keep handling breaking news, when the information is unscripted and events are changing quickly. News Anchors in smaller markets may do a substantial amount of writing and producing the daily news show. Some do daily reporting, as well. In large markets anchors spend less time writing and producing news while spending more time at community events, being the face of the station. An anchor's story telling skills may erode as they are less often required to go out in the field. Experience often compensates for the lack of regular reporting when they are called upon to tell a story for sweeps or a special project.

The best anchors communicate smoothly in all phases, the rest make a fairly big noise. Most of the time anchors read from teleprompters in air conditioned studios, and that's not too tough. I know because I've anchored at every station I've worked. It is fun and exciting. There is some glory and a few ego strokes, too. All without the effort required for general assignment reporting. Who wouldn't like that kind of job? I'm always looking for more.

## Engineers

When your gear doesn't work right or the computer freezes up, who you gonna call? Engineers put out the proverbial hardware fires we ignite in the field and inside the building.

Another critically important player to producing quality news, engineers don't usually get a lot of attention. They are background guys. That's their personality, too. Most do not have strict engineering degrees, but arrive at their position in television through job experience. Besides fixing cameras, computers and the multitude of devices that break down daily at every TV station, these guys work on towers, fixing antennae, receivers, transmitters and other difficult, slightly hairy stuff. We rarely see them doing that.

Surprisingly, there are few women engineers in TV news.

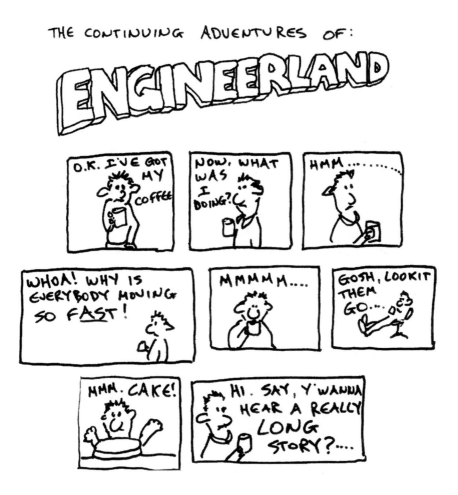

Engineers don't like the bustle and last minute nature of news so they don't hang around the newsroom much. Their method is different. Trouble shooting is a process of elimination or following steps in order. Hurrying is not their preferred work method, but they are usually quite capable of fixing something in a jiffy.

## Editors

In newsroom hierarchy, editors like writers are underappreciated, but necessary to a well produced news show. They too, fly beneath the radar. But when the sewage is flowing it can pool up under an editor's door. Editors regularly bail out needy producers and disorganized newsrooms. They are the last line of defense before a black hole or breaking news gaffe. So it is a more stressful job than writer but not quite as stressful as producing. When news breaks quickly, it may be <u>the</u> most stressful job in the building. Taking a feed from the helicopter or live truck then editing it to air as soon as possible with a news director looking over your shoulder causes perspiration just writing it. Editors rarely get awards or a pat on the back, yet they are integral to getting a show on the air. When a show is "clean", editors have a big hand in that.

Editors make less than producers but more than writers. They may belong to unions in larger markets.

## Helicopter Pilots

A specialized field, flying news helicopters is a dangerous job. It's stressful, too. Because flying is expensive, news directors can have unrealistic expectations about what a helicopter should be able to do. This is the usual conflict. Newsrooms want to fly places or in conditions professional pilots deem unsafe.

You want to fly with a pilot who insists on safety, appropriate flying conditions and is in constant communication with the other pilots around him in the sky. You don't want to fly with a cowboy trying to out fly the other news choppers: flying too low or avoiding radio communication with them. That's when accidents happen and accidents involving helicopters are beyond bad.

Not to paint with a too broad brush. Between us we've flown with just five. All guys. Their background isn't journalism. They don't hang around the newsroom unless they're required to. Personalities differ. The only common denominator is they enjoy toys like Harleys, jet skis, boats, cars and adrenaline.

They are a little apart from the rest of us, too. Aviators seem to prefer the company of other aviators. It's a select group for the most part that doesn't usually include news people. Unless they have a boat, a jet ski or a Harley.

People on the ground in the newsroom who bark at pilots and get them agitated are a real nuisance when you're flying. There is no worse feeling than watching your pilot lose his temper in an argument with the desk while you sit helpless in the back seat 500 feet high.

Shooting from the helicopter is straightforward. Get the tightest shots possible of the subject. If the situation is dynamic, like a car chase, just stay with it. No cutaways or wide shots while the action is happening; if something exciting happens, you must be tight when it does. If you're shooting a static scene, like a car accident, shoot the different elements as tight as possible, then get a wide shot. If you're live, then stick with the action the whole time and zoom out slowly at the end of the shot.

Flying is fun. The first few times you fly are a rush. Made me want to buy a Harley. There's just that nagging fraction of a chance that something might happen. You need to think about it if you have a family or any flying fear. At our shop, about three quarters of the photographers like to fly.

Flying is reserved for larger markets that can afford it and where helicopters are required to compete. Fortunately, the market in which Monty and I ply our trade is big enough. And I love it. I have always enjoyed flying—planes, little planes, and now helicopters. I'd never flown in a helicopter until I arrived in my current situation. Now I look to go up whenever I can. We have an excellent pilot. He's young, but has plenty of experience, ability, and most important, good sense. I feel safe. I love the view a helicopter affords. The expensive camera on board gets amazing pictures. There is always the element of risk in all that we do, but I feel as safe in our helicopter as I do driving down the highway in a Ford Explorer. The helicopter is much, much faster.

# Writers

News writers are either producers in the making, former producers who prefer less stress, or occasionally interns. News writers are rarely noticed (Nice job on that vosot!), yet good writers contribute to well-produced news: re-writing wire stories, cranking out vosots and teases. They work in the newsroom around producers, but generally avoid the same pressures. Good writers get recognized and promoted to producer, if they wish. Average writers may be allowed to languish for years in that capacity. Less creative than the title suggests. Writers are paid about the least of permanent newsroom positions. Undervalued.

In some shops, writer positions are being cut to save the small salary they make. This is unfortunate. It adds to the producer's workload, giving them less time to write good teases, work with field crews or craft their show. The elimination of writers hobbles reporters, too. Writers often condense reporter-written stories for later shows, or take care of that pesky v. o., so reporters can concentrate on larger pieces. A good writer is a friend to many in the newsroom. A mediocre writer is better than nothing. My shop got rid of all its writers to the detriment of our product.

# Assignment Desk

Sometimes called "assignment editors" or "assignment managers", these people are neither fish nor flesh. They don't produce any part of the news yet are vital in the gathering of it. They tell you with whom you're working, your destination, whom you'll meet there and often when you will take lunch. They are a fulcrum around which the news day pivots. They may move you to a different story when you're in the middle of something you've worked hard on. Breaking news happens. This can be frustrating, but is rarely the fault of the assignment desk.

They typically echo a producer or news director's wishes. They have information when you need it: a contact, phone number, address or help in general. The best perform all these functions with a sense of humor and appreciation of how things work in the field. In the order of pay, assignment editors are paid more than photographers, but less than an executive producer or assistant news director.

Really good news outfits have a solid desk. Less reliable assignment editors are a screwdriver in the spokes, undermining in little ways: giving inaccurate information, distracting with unnecessary phone calls, creating extra work when you're slammed. Death from a thousand cuts. Some wear the invisible uniform of mediocrity when they blame co-workers to avoid responsibility for problems they created. Sad, but fairly common in this position. Good assignment editors help crews arrive at outcomes smoothly.

This is another stressful position beholden to the news director, executive producer or whoever's in charge. These folks wear a head set all day and spend most of it on the phone and computer. With everyone asking for stuff, there's rarely a stroke of appreciation for the multi-tasking desk manager because the job entails so many little things. But a really efficient news desk is broadly appreciated as a team asset. Reporters can be local superstars, break big stories and tell stories. Photographers can tell stories, too. Assignment desk managers don't receive that recognition, but they can make important contributions to a top-flight news operation.

## Interns

Interns are usually university journalism students who want to get their feet wet. It is the best first step for anyone interested in a television news career. Depending on the station and market size, interns might be called upon to write stories like vosots or readers, the kind of work that news writers perform. Most interns are attracted to the sparkle of on-air reporting or what they perceive to be a glamorous profession. A few hours driving around on some dingy crime story will remove some of the luster. That's good. Job shadowing is the best way to decide whether or not to give TV news a try. Driving around with a news crew once a week shows impressionable interns how un-glamorous it is.

Interns should remember, TV news people in most markets work <u>hard</u> for an income that might be less than a waiter earns in a nice restaurant downtown. Smart interns consider all of this before they get into news for fortune and fame.

At the same time, many find the job shadow intriguing and the work interesting. This job is interesting. It makes sense, upon graduation, to send the tape you made during the internship to stations in small markets and try to make an impression with the news director. That's typically how young people get started.

Most of us remember our first station fondly. And especially the people we worked with there. For many, this is <u>the</u> formative experience of our career. Exciting, but difficult. That is because small market photographers and reporters often perform both jobs.

## Sports

The one word title belies the intriguing and changing role this department plays in most TV news operations. Many news directors in markets smaller than the thirty major cities home to professional sports franchises would like to eliminate their sports department. Even in the cities with professional teams, news operations consider covering sports a burden which doesn't add to the bottom line. Twenty four hour sports networks, each teams respective web site, independent sports web sites cover the subject much better than most local TV news operations and their ever decreasing resources. What Red Sox fan outside the Boston TV market, relies on their local TV news to deliver the latest scores and player updates? That's the rub. Local TV news sports departments can only satisfy casual fans of the local teams.

Your TV sports report can deliver something ESPN cannot and that's the profile of an interesting local athlete, team or event. These stories can be personal, amusing or even heart-breaking. Athletic competition has a lot of human emotion wrapped up in it. As the best news stories involve people and emotion, so can stories about local high school athletes, competitors in less popular sports or amazing athletic feats performed by local people. The best local TV news sports departments deliver these visual, emotional stories even while their bosses consider them dispensable.

## Web Staff

This one of the few areas of local TV newsrooms that has seen a general increase in hiring. As a station's web presence becomes more important, a competent web staff is seen as essential to staying competitive.

The average viewer's news habit has changed. They no longer wait for the five o'clock news to discover the day's events in their city. And if that news viewer does not subscribe to the city newspaper, his best option for local information before the news hour will be his favorite TV news website. It's difficult to overestimate the importance of this source for information because we get more hits every day.

The people who write the reports and keep the website running are skilled in several seemingly unrelated areas, computers and writing. While reporters often provide the copy for the web version of their story, stations that have the best websites rely on their web staff to do most of the writing. The majority of people in this department have a background in Information Technology and Computer Science. They may have little experience with journalism and writing for news. But most website stories are paraphrased, so the web writers pick it up quickly. They are not expected to produce writing at the level of newspapers or magazines. While TV news website stories are generally shorter than the next day's newspaper version, they can inform nearly as well. This seems to meet the expectations of TV news website consumers. How much is that New York Times web subscription?

## Chasing the Weather

TV stations love to cover the weather. <u>Really</u> love it. And for good reason. Viewers tune in for weather coverage. They want to know if school is delayed. Which roads are icy? Will flooding, freezing or heat mess up their plans? So we go crazy for weather coverage. The battle cry goes out. Live Storm Team Coverage. The problem is that it gets out of hand. When you start crying wolf and continue to cry wolf, it damages credibility. Working in the Pacific Northwest, we see our share of wet weather, along with some snow and ice. It is expected. Yet we still go nuts when the precipitation begins every year, and usually keep it up until the sun finally shines again in June. At times like these, weather can seem like the discourse of fools.

I once spent two days covering, or should I say, chasing the weather. Day One was freezing fog, sending us an hour south. It wasn't there. During our live shots we talked about freezing fog the prior weekend, implying that it was out there still and drivers needed to be cautious, even a little fearful. We offered some driving tips. Stuff everybody knows. Tap dancing on non-weather events can be embarrassing. At least, we had video of a car accident from the weekend to cover my face.

Day Two, freezing rain, half hour west. But there is none to be found. We went live anyway, using video of an overnight crash on an icy road well outside town. Warning drivers again to be watchful for the freezing rain we were unable to locate and about which we had no reliable information. Ridiculous. Worse still, we had to drive two hours in the opposite direction to a freeway closed for icy conditions. By the time we got there, the ice had melted. No closure, no problems. We were live at noon, the sun hitting my face, making something out of nothing again. And doing it very well, I might add. It comes with practice. This is the life of a reporter in a weather crazy business. People will watch, until they get sick of coverage of non-events, or normal weather. I love covering a good storm, just not the little ones. A word of warning to journalism students interested in this career. If you work in local news, you will cover routine storms and normal weather events as major news stories.

That Tim's station occasionally pushes weather stories when conditions aren't severe is not unusual. There is a reason. Viewers consistently reveal in focus groups they watch the local news for weather information before anything else. Indeed, this is a useful, public service we provide in times of dangerous weather.

The other day, after the competition's meteorologist forecast a big storm four or five days out, the news director and executive producer met with our chief meteorologist to see if we could begin forecasting the same information. This kind of news is good for ratings. People tune in to see when the big storm will hit. If it's big enough for Live Storm Team Coverage, ratings increase. People stay home to watch while the snowfall accumulates outside. But four or five days out, weather is very tricky to predict, unless you're in San Diego.

Our chief weather guy, Rod was in this place of precarious prediction. He's a serious meteorologist who enjoys his work. This day he was conflicted. You don't want to be wrong about a prediction and forecast an event that never comes to pass. At the same time, when your boss says he'd like to start reporting the big storm channel eight is predicting, it's tough. No human knows exactly what the weather will be four or five days out. And Rod was not substituting a capital G for the first letter in his name.

By that evening, Rod began forecasting a large Pacific storm and strong winds. As predicted, it blew in and was severe enough to knock over whole hillsides of trees and cause widespread power blackouts. In this case, the public was served (the portion anyway that pays attention to local TV weather) and at least two chief meteorologists kept their job.

The flip side to this service and accurate weather prediction in general is meteorologists taping forecasts at 7 a. m. for airing at noon without acknowledging that the information is five hours old. This trend in medium size markets and smaller is a cost cutter because it frees up meteorologists to go out and report after taping the noon forecast. As the accuracy of meteorological prediction erodes so might viewer's trust in local TV news generally. To a lot of business people upstairs, this trade off is fair. And so, profit margin trumps accuracy in news. This is probably when a news director needs to draw a journalistic line in the sand instead of telling the morning weather guy to go out and turn a couple of vosots before they leave.

## Galaxy Eleven

Microwave or satellite truck operation may seem ancillary to the business of photojournalism. In fact, reporters, photographers and truck operators are bound together in breaking news and most live shots. The story won't get fed in time to make its slot unless all three perform.

An unsung hero in breaking news situations, the best truck engineers are motivated to help news crews create good live shots. They are savvy, curious, intelligent technicians with a blue-collar approach. Trained to be calm and safe when things get crazy, truck engineers keep a clear head during breaking news opportunities. That can be a relief for crews who feel they are managing chaos. How about the trick of hitting a satellite the size of a mini-van 22,000 miles above the equator with a bullseye?

The truck "op" will find a safe location for the live truck that's near enough to the story so the live shot makes sense. That distance can be several hundred feet because most live trucks carry several 200 foot spools of cable. He will run cable and electricity to the spot you select. If the cable run isn't too far, he may be able to set up a light for photogs busy editing in the truck.

While finding the safest spot near the live shot is the first consideration, live truck drivers know a good live shot doesn't distract other drivers or traffic. We've seen our share of rubberneckers slamming on the brakes.

Live trucks and their loud graphics add a wrinkle of grief to friends and family of the recently deceased. We should be as sensitive to the aggrieved as we would our own neighbors in the same circumstances. Experienced truck engineers find discreet locations to work from when conditions allow it. Sometimes this is logistically impossible. In the case of the Oregon City girls, Ashley Pond and Miranda Gaddis, both girls were found murdered near a busy intersection and the media assembled there for most of the week. Every driver slowed down to look at the house and field the girls were found in, the cluster of live trucks and a fence memorial packed with mourners dropping off balloons, teddy bears and letters of grief. It was an outdoor circus to which the national and local media added their own touches. We may even have encouraged it. Afterwards, numerous locals told me the big media presence made the tragedy worse. I heard the same thing from affected students after the Thurston High shooting in Springfield, Oregon. It's not our job as journalists to try to make people feel better. But we can keep a lower profile and have some consideration for the aggrieved while still doing our work. Experienced live trucks engineers, a local TV news species on the brink of extinction, have a developed sense for these situations.

## Photojournalists as Live Truck Operators

Increasingly, photojournalists are required to run live trucks. This is particularly true in small and medium size markets. It's a skill set that needs regular refreshment. But performing it more than once a week gets to be a drag for serious photojournalists.

Stories generally turn out better when the photographer concentrates on shooting and editing her story without microwave shot and safety concerns. Unions call it "separation of duties". They don't appreciate overlap. I do not know a single photojournalist who doesn't prefer an engineer to run the truck and help set up the live shot. And it's much safer. Photographers who gather and edit a story of suitable quality for broadcast news, while setting up a remote microwave truck safely and quickly are being asked to do a lot. Safety gets compromised when it's one job among several. Often the person telling you to hustle out to shoot, edit, set up the truck and feed back in time for a live shot has never done this job themselves nor could they. Or they may be years removed from the experience and have conveniently forgotten what is required. For safety's sake, you should not be bullied or pressured into a dangerous live shot. Insist on safety for yourself and your reporter.

But you had better be careful. Complaining about running a live truck can get you labeled a malcontent rather than someone devoted to their craft. That said, when you're feeling more "truck op" than photojournalist, tell the news director. Whether they care or bother to do anything about it, is a fair measure of any news department. Because it's possible no one in management is concerned whether you're reaching your professional goals, or not. And that is a professional dead end. Currently, my boss requires we write down our professional goals and expects us to meet them. This is good and fairly unusual. If you're the type of photographer who doesn't want to get stuck running a live truck all the time, it's important to ask during job interviews what are your potential employer's expectations regarding photojournalists operating live trucks.

## Never Mix Lightning and Live Shots

The humidity in the Pacific Northwest isn't muggy like the east coast. Our summers are mild by comparison. We do get some crazy electrical storms around the mountain tops though.

One summer day in Eugene, I was dispatched to a hill above the MacKenzie River. As I raised the mast, I spied some clouds over a distant hill, dark as steel wool. Over the years, I've seen a lot of thunder storms emanating from clouds like these. I called the meteorologist who relayed some information from his computer models. There was indeed lightning occurring, but well south of us. Around this time, I heard a low rumble from up the valley. I was a little spooked and thought my safety around this fifty foot mast was in question. So I dropped the mast and stepped away from the truck. Light rain was falling silently on the dusty hilltop when a blinding flash lit the scene in an instant of bright relief. Thunder was instantaneous, deafening and right overhead. I fell to my knees immediately and remained kneeling in the dirt for awhile. Eventually, I jumped into the live truck and radioed the desk about this frightening near miss and scuttled live shot. They were not happy at all and reminded me the live shot was minutes away.

The first objective for a photojournalist or engineer asked to run live trucks is to come home alive at the end of the day. You are responsible for yourself, your reporter and anyone standing near the truck. No story or breaking news event is worth pushing a microwave mast into power lines or risking electrocution in a lightning storm.

Every few years, somebody in our little fraternity of photojournalists, reporters and live truck operators gets electrocuted. Some die. Surviving electrocution is not pretty, either. I've met a survivor and it was heart breaking to see how he and his family's life had changed very much for the worse. The best way to avoid the very real dangers encountered running live trucks is to develop a safety checklist for yourself, just like a photographer's trick bag. Here are mine.

1. Be familiar with any truck you operate. If you haven't run a truck in a few months, find an engineer familiar with the truck and have her go over its operation with you. It should only take a few minutes to remind yourself of the main points and get back a safety edge.

2. Arrive at the live shot location as early as possible to avoid being rushed. Park in the safest, level spot, away from power lines and obstructions; but near enough to run cable to the location. It's always better to park in a safe spot. Even if you have to spend more time running cable.

3. After you've parked, walk around and away from the truck. Look up for power lines or tree obstructions. The mast should be well free of any swaying tree branches. Power lines must be more than ten feet away from the nearest part of the mast. In windy conditions, that distance should increase based on the sway of the mast or lines. I try to park further than the mast's radius from any power lines. That is not always possible. If it's too dark and you can't quite see, DO NOT extend the mast. That's crazy, brother. No live shot is worth taking that chance. Sometimes you just have to tell the desk, it's not safe and you can't get a shot out. On the other hand, can you get a signal out without putting up the mast? Is there some spot with line of sight to the receiving tower? Perhaps you might move to a safer spot and still get the shot out?

4. If the location is safe, you may need to level the vehicle by popping a tire up on a curb or using levelers. Be careful in leveling that it does not move the mast nearer lines or obstructions when you raise it.

5. If you are ready to raise the mast, watch it as it goes up. This is the step during which most fatal accidents happen. Do not be distracted.

6. Once extended, take another look to make sure the mast's position is where it should be. Occasionally, the mast will be nearer obstacles than originally planned. You might need to make the difficult decision of lowering the mast and

moving to a better spot. If the mast is too close for comfort, make the decision to move quickly. It's best to find the safest, best location at the outset to avoid moving.

7. Make sure the mast's alarm system works well. Every year 6-10 satellite antennas and, at least, 20 mast tops are broken off because of damaged or disabled mast alarms.

When the live shot is done, stow the mast carefully. Walk around the vehicle again to make sure you haven't forgotten anything and doors and panels are closed tightly.

This last section is not a complete course for safe live truck operation. The details of how to perform in emergency situations is best described in the literature and videos that deal specifically with that subject. Study them. More detailed microwave and satellite truck safety guidelines are available through your state. We have OSHA here in Oregon and they have useful suggestions. The dalai lama of live truck safety is Mark Bell, publisher of the "ENG Safety Newsletter". I've had the privilege of attending a workshop of Mark's at the NPPA Conference in 2001. His work is dedicated to keeping news crews and electronic news gathering in general as safe as can be. Mark may be reached at 1URSAFE-6090. Thanks for everything you do, Mark.

It is upsetting to see specialization knocked out of our business by a model that wants more from everyone for less. In better times and larger markets, technicians ran microwave live trucks, allowing reporter/photographer teams to focus on getting the story. At my station, truck technicians went away several years ago. Photojournalists were trained to run the satellite trucks and we've relied on them to do this ever since. Now they go with a reporter in the truck, get the story, edit it, and then are expected to tune in to the big bird in the sky and do the live shot without straying more than 10 feet (the necessary cable length) from the truck. Whew! Calling this double duty is insufficient to describe the skill set. More importantly, the quality of the news product we're feeding back can be extremely limited. This in a day when live shots reign supreme. Live, local and late-breaking was one station's mantra. But this two-person live newsroom is hard pressed to report all the story elements because of the other jobs they must perform. They haven't the flexibility to set up their live shots wherever they wish or even as quickly as they would like in breaking news situations because they are likely out gathering the story. The FCC should frown on this for safety reasons alone. I think many managers know the value of specialized truck operators, but once cut from budgets they are rarely re-hired. Sadly, sharing this perspective with the bosses can get you labeled lazy.

Microwave truck operators create the ability to do higher quality news coverage at live locations, freeing the photographer and reporter to move as necessary to the most advantageous viewpoint.

Microwave truck operators also create a safer work environment for everyone including the general public who like to hang around during live shots.

Boo on the bean counters upstairs!

Given this unfortunate work reality, it is more important than ever for that two person crew to be a team. Reporters, be ready to get your hands dirty, and probably your slacks, too. Do your primary responsibilities, but then be ready to pull cable, set up a light—whatever it takes. It's not so bad, and will keep you from turning into a prima donna. As long as your pants are dirty, help break down the shot too. You will win friends. I speak from experience, having spent a few years doing the morning live shot routine. It seems you are always throwing up live shots. Doing it together is good practice any time. Too bad it's become a daily expectation.

## Don't Become the Story

Reporters and photographers often end up out in the weather, on the side of the road, or knocking on a stranger's door. This can be dangerous business if you aren't paying attention, and sometimes when you are. It's important in the excitement of the moment to be aware of your surroundings, and remove yourself from situations that pose a threat to your safety. We're not saying call off the live shot in the wind storm or on the side of the road. Crews in the field solving journalistic, engineering and safety problems simultaneously need to take precautions and choose the best locations they can. If it's too risky, don't do it. You work as a team. Watch the other guy's back.

A recent January storm brought tornado force winds to the coast. There was a lot of damage, and we were there to cover it. It was an exciting opportunity to report a real weather event. A little scary at times, there was some risk involved. But we watched out for each other and nobody got hurt. I was with a great photographer named Dale Birkholz, who's been shooting news for decades. We were on the south side of Newport, Oregon with the highway under three feet of water. The wind was whipping hard enough to knock you over.

With permission from a state trooper, we stopped in the road beyond the point where civilian vehicles were being re-routed. We needed pictures of the flooded highway, trees blowing sideways and toppling. We got the great video, including trees falling literally at our feet. My job was to help Dale any way I could so he could get these shots and then get out. Mostly, I watched out for anything falling or blowing our way. Whether you're a local news crew covering a wind storm or an embedded New York Times reporter riding in a humvee around Baghdad, being aware and reacting to what you see can keep you from getting hurt or killed.

Recently, a very unsettling thing happened to one of our crews.

I came in to work a night side shift, filling in for a 2:30 p.m. start. Shortly after I arrived, I heard I would be live in our early newscasts at a scene where a driver intentionally smashed his car into a radio station lobby. Then he left the scene.

Nobody was hurt, but they easily could have been. The guy rammed his car most of the way into the building and moved the large reception desk a foot. Glass and debris flew everywhere. We learned from the radio folks that they believed this was a disturbed and angry listener, who had been sending violent e-mails to the station for years but had never acted on them. This day he did. They got his license plate, and so did police. So did we.

As I learned of my assignment that day, I also learned that we had sent a crew to the address of the vehicle owner. Not only did we have a crew near the suspect's home, but that crew had talked to the man, and it was all on tape. They went up to his door and knocked. Given the circumstances, this was an extremely risky thing to do. Our news room's confrontation of a mentally ill and apparently violent offender was a bone-headed play. The reporter went to the door of a guy who two hours before had slammed his car into a radio station lobby due to his rage at the media and mental imbalance. Then we waltz up to his door to check in with him? Not smart. A relatively inexperienced reporter was encouraged by the assignment editor to do it. She called to ask what to do and was advised to talk to him. This is the most worrisome aspect of the episode.

It turned into a very scary encounter. The man yelled, cursed, flailed his arms, got in the reporter's face while the photographer (also young and new to the station) taped from behind a tree. At one point, the man told the reporter to wait while he went to his car to get something. He eventually brought her a crazy manifesto he'd written, but what if he'd returned with a gun?

Eventually, the station called police, and nobody got hurt. Detectives were amazed at what we did. So am I. Yes, we got there first. Yes, we got exclusive video of a crazy man. And yes, someone could have been hurt or killed. What amazes me still is the lack of understanding in our newsroom. Even after the fact, we didn't see the danger inherent in this brand of news gathering. The smart thing would have been to confirm the plate number, keep a safe distance and call police. You still get exclusive video of the arrest without risking anyone's personal safety which, were it to happen, would have become the story.

## Keep It Loose

A news room can be tense. Producers, editors and writers are fairly tethered to their space, so uptight newsrooms are especially hard for them. Not accidentally. Some bosses want to keep everyone on their toes. In a tire shop, this may work. But news rooms, like hospitals and police stations are very stressful places. Not to imply that we are saving lives or protecting innocents. A news room is like a boiler plate at times. A boss who likes to turn up the heat does a disservice to the people in her employ. When things are kept loose, news rooms can be efficient with good ideas flying around and a lot of creativity. The shows usually reflect it. That kind of atmosphere in a TV news room is exceptional.

There's an apt analogy for our business. It's about the frog in the boiling pot. Toss a frog into a boiling pot of water and he will instantly jump out, singed but not boiled. Put a frog into a pot of tepid water and he will remain. Now turn up the heat. In as long as it takes water to boil, you will have your boiled frog. So it is with people. They'll tolerate great discomfort if they grow accustomed to it, even risking their health. Many people who land in news without any prior experience jump out fairly soon. It's the kind of work that takes getting used to because most newsroom managers confuse running a tight ship with an uptight one. Relax, you guys. Stop frowning at good ideas and encourage originality by taking a chance with stories.

# Unions

In many medium to large TV markets, unions represent photographers and, slightly less often, reporters, anchors, editors and engineers. By represent we mean help negotiate contracts, advise management about work conditions and provide a buffer between labor and management. How unions function exactly is complex. We thought it would be useful to discuss how unions affect our work place. They can be important if you want a raise, working conditions are unsafe and so on.

At my shop, we are members of International Cinematographer's Guild, the union out of Hollywood, California. Dues are fairly dear, I pay over $200 a year. Some of my co-workers chaff about union dues. The union has helped me out once when a co-worker and I were unfairly terminated. We returned to work with back pay after two long months. In a nutshell the union convinced management they couldn't fire me for a traffic violation that was thrown out of court. It sounds silly now, but it was worrisome for my wife and me. Handled fairly insensitively, just before he took my key pass and a metal door slammed behind me, the N. D. offered this advice, "As some doors close, others will open."

I doubt without the union's persuasion, that same news director would have felt compelled to welcome me back. In time, everything returned to normal. Nevertheless, it takes the strength of a union to help workers stand up to some bosses in this business.

At my shop, NABET (National Association of Broadcast Engineers and Technicians) represents photographers, editors, master control operators, and assignment desk and website workers. In my opinion, the union has served these employees well over the past few years of ownership and changes in benefits. Union leadership has confronted station policy and actions, filing grievances to right wrongs and force the company to honor contract stipulations. In almost every case, arbitrators ruled in the union's favor.

The union also negotiated a contract that on balance rewards workers in terms of pay and benefits better than those without a bargaining unit. Union workers get a much better deal for over-time, short turnaround pay, and added holidays than the rest of us. An effort to organize on-air workers at our station a few years back failed by one vote. The further that decision fades in memory, the more regrettable it feels.

## Are We Covering the Story Or Just Covering Our Butt?

When a news room finds itself playing catch up to a story they saw the competition doing first, the straggler will often run some video of the event or some file video that fits the story and call it good. It goes like this:

Q: Hey, did we get that big story?

A: Yeah, we ran a v. o. on it at 6:30.

This is how producers and sometimes news rooms protect themselves when they're slow getting to a story. By running the v. o. as soon as possible, producers have an excuse if they get called into the office. In theory, it makes sense. It's pro-active. You're cut-ting your losses. But if you choose to ignore the story because you got beat initially, you hurt yourself by short-changing viewers.

## Nature of the Beast

While it's a good thing to be confident and ambitious in this business, one's head can swell from self-importance. This is true on several levels. Individually, collectively and institution-ally, people get too full of themselves. Here's a story, related by a polite, talented, ambitious reporter who would never do damage to another, if she could help it. She did something on the job that she was uncomfortable about.

Recently around town, there had been a number of run-ins between motorists and cyclists on the city streets. Establishing their turf, so to speak, some of these road rage arguments turned violent. No one died, but some people were hurt. Curiously, it was the automobile drivers taking the brunt of punishment. This July, a delivery van driver got knocked unconscious by a few cyclists who thought he wasn't respecting their right-of-way.

We got pretty worked up about this potential news story. Portland is a bike-friendly city. The recent spate of arguments got the public's attention. Also, bike enthusiasts represent a demographic (age 20 to 35) advertisers covet. So when the incident involving the delivery van occurred, the news room got excited.

The van's driver took a few stitches and headed home to rest up for his next day of work. During those few hours, several stations were able to find him and get some sound, or as we refer to it:

an interview with the victim. My co-worker arrived at the victim's house in time to see a colleague from another station (channel eight, of course) leaving. Assuming the competition had beaten her to the interview, she was anxious for an interview herself.

Arriving at the door, the trucker's wife said her husband was asleep, resting up for his shift in five hours and still smarting from the stitches (and perhaps the humiliation of being knocked out by two skinny bicyclists with their pant legs rolled up.)

Sensing that not getting the interview might land her in the news director's office, our reporter begged the wife.

"I just need two minutes with your husband, please."

But his wife would not have it. Her husband was tired, beat up and needing rest so he could return to his job in a few hours. My colleague pulled her trump card.

"Look", she said. "If I don't get this interview, I'm going to have to explain it to my boss and may get fired." Possibly, but not likely. The wife was moved, however. She awakened her husband. The interview was gathered and one reporter (and photographer) kept their jobs that day. But at what cost? A few weeks later, we both agreed people had lost interest in the story almost completely. But in the moment it all seemed very important. The news room's needs seemed paramount. The question we raised was this:

"Why did we put this poor guy through all that grief for something no one remembered the next week?" She summed it up this way.

"It's the nature of the beast."

In retrospect, she might have handled it differently. An interview with the wife and photograph of her husband might have told the story almost as well. But not if channel eight had his stitched up face crying about the beating he took. It's hard to accept less than you perceive the competition is getting. This is when the Beast has escaped its cage and usually refuses to return to it. It's one of the moral dilemmas specific to TV news. You do what you have to do to keep your job, even though the job givers wouldn't be caught dead in your shoes.

## The Number Two

The assistant news director, sometimes called an executive producer (slight pejorative), can be more than a figurehead or vice president. Of course, their effectiveness and influence in the direction of quality news product depends on their boss. Secure news directors don't leash their #2 and let them help as much as they can. Assistant news directors with something to offer can without intending be the rock of a news room. They don't have quite the same set of expectations as their boss, so they might work more closely and better with crews. They might also have a different and better vision than the big guy in the corner office. This is the best case scenario for any newsroom—an E. P. with a news director's vision.

## The Uniform of Mediocrity

Good managers and bosses are leaders. Good managers motivate people by working with them to be the best reporter, anchor, producer, photojournalist they can be. And not only because other people's success reflects well on them. Good managers have a genuine interest in the people they employ. People working for them want to go in the direction they are leading.

All leaders do not have to be well-liked. It helps if they are liked, at least nominally, for the sake of morale. People want to follow someone they admire. But effective leaders who inspire successful news outfits need not be loved by their troops. A real hard ass with a clear vision and ability to get their message across can still get the whole boat pulling as one.

As we said, it's easier to criticize the boss than be her. That said, there are plenty of challenged bosses and managers in TV newsrooms. But pilgrims have grievances.

There are managers who work on maintaining a Teflon-coat which allows them to shed anything negative, appear clean while doing little to improve the end product. None of these qualities translate into being a good manager of people, let alone a leader.

It should be said challenged managers do not inhabit newsrooms exclusively. They are everywhere, of course. But the glare of their deficiencies shines especially in a news setting.

Another trait, not exclusive to news, but mediocre managers everywhere is the tendency to give people extra work so the managers will have less. This shift of responsibility is sometimes referred to as "delegating". It's doubtful that fits the Webster's definition.

Another management style employs the dual approach of rarely giving feedback until someone messes up then hammering down. The Wack-a-Mole Method is prevalent in newsrooms or any workplace where managers think motivation comes from discouragement.

A boss whose news instincts or character are doubted by his staff will have a hard time. People recognize a ship without much rudder. Pity the hindsight Einstein whose feedback is mainly fault finding. One symptom is a mad scramble to assign blame before figuring out what to do next. Blame storming. When managers fall into this mode, one may watch all the smaller boats in the newsroom navigating away from the tempest.

## When the Whip Comes Down

Seven words you don't want to hear at work: "There are going to be some changes."

That is how it went at my work place, anyway. The station I work for has been sold again. Owned by a small group, backed by a private equity firm with deep pockets, the previous ownership lasted a year and a half, during which time twenty one people were laid off. A dozen more left after that. The few replacements are younger, less experienced and cheaper. Our news production has been automated and requires fewer people. It's an inflexible "system" which, after initially delivering many newscasts to a glitch-filled Hell, has become consistently mediocre in its presentation: clipped audio, confused-looking anchors, stories not airing properly, less breaking news capability. Our engineering staff is cut to the bone. Equipment is in disrepair. Cameras and live trucks are literally falling apart.

Now a new ownership group has ridden in promising to improve the situation, add back, not cut more. But that's what the last guys said. So we'll see. This group is also a small one, backed by private equity money and private investors looking for a big return. So far, they have just slightly improved our health care coverage. Today, we had a 401k information meeting. What sort of match may we expect? Zero.

We can only hope our news coverage improves more than the incremental gain in health care for ourselves and our families. Will we continue to do the cheapest news possible, or will we return to offering viewers something substantial? Stay tuned, if you can stand it.

## Where's Our Golden Parachute?

CEOs of communications companies as a rule make lavish salaries. Whatever additional revenue may be generated from lower overhead often finds its way into executive's pockets in the form of bonuses or easy incentives. Stockholders or investors usually agree with this system and pay structure as long as their return on investment is good. The trouble is that few if any of these individuals have a long term interest. Investors get out when economic winds shift. Executives move on to other companies and positions whenever it's advantageous to their career. Nothing wrong with a person improving their situation. The problem is when an operation goes into free fall, these same CEOs bail out with "golden parachutes": a grand ransom in the form of severance pay.

Slightly lower down the food chain, news directors who deliver poor ratings and get fired usually have similar severance payouts worked into their contracts. We're not against anyone working the best deal they can for themselves and their family. But if it's fair for a news director, than why not a producer, reporter or writer? Aren't they in trouble when they lose their jobs? News room foot soldiers rarely receive any severance or pay out when let go. And underlings usually get fired for less costly errors than bringing a corporation to financial ruin or dragging down ratings.

## Distinguish Yourself

Good news outfits take chances when they have an opportunity to overtake the competition. You don't win the ratings game playing it safe. Or playing to avoid losing. Trying to be more like the number one station is a terrible strategy. So it is that managers afraid to take chances with stories usually wind up in third place. Merely encouraging news rooms to "think outside the box" is not the same as out-thinking the competition.

You have to take chances and calculated risks with story choices. Make important stories important to viewers by giving them a longer treatment. Important sweeps stories should have a look and feel that distinguishes them from the day turn stories. Different angles of successful sweeps stories should be followed up and presented to viewers who are following it. The presentation of longer format stories must have a solid journalistic foundation of giving both sides and letting viewers decide, showing and telling them things they don't already know. The best way to improve ratings with the team and resources at hand is to tell better stories that are important to viewers.

Viewers may take more than a year to respond to whatever style, direction and approach your newsroom is offering. Consistency of vision is crucial to moving viewers and ratings. But winning will be difficult if the door to the news director's office is revolving. It doesn't matter what stations are selling with their particular brand and news style, changing it every time a new news director replaces the old news director will only confuse the few viewers you can keep.

It's hard to win with disgruntled players. It happens, but rarely.

Besides consistency of vision and doing original stories, treating your people right can have a direct effect on news product, too.

## Balancing your Life

TV News will take a lot of your time and energy. If you start your career as a young, single person, you won't mind working hard and partying harder when you can. It worked that way for me early on. But like any demanding profession, eventually your personal time gets pinched the older you get. Lots of people work hard, long hours. But TV news is definitely one of the more *time consuming*. The news cycle is 24 hours long and, increasingly, the business demands you fill more of it. There's little down time whatever shift you work and stories take their toll, physically and emotionally.

A typical dayside schedule may not begin until 9 a.m., but often stretches to 7 p.m. Frequently, lunch fits in as you're driving, on the way back from wherever you've been, logging sound or before writing for the evening 'casts. There's a lot of hurry up and wait, but don't count on a half hour lunch break.

Especially as you grow older and build a family, the demands on your home life seem to conflict with pressures at work. You will need to find some balance. Recognize the challenge. Enjoy your family as much as you can. Have a hobby (like fly fishing!) and make sure you take the time off you deserve. The newsroom may make you feel like you owe it even more. But recognize that work cannot be the only facet of your life, or it will kill you. Work hard but don't let it grind you down. . . or it will.

## The Nearest, Faraway Place

Tim's desire to balance his sometimes draining work schedule with something meaningful is common in TV news. A lot of people we work with practice hobbies at a very high level. Tim's a trout conservationist. His conservation strategy is spooking fish to the other side of the lake where no one can catch them. For most of us in news, weekends are necessary to recharge your battery, hit the reset button or just check out. You may find refuge in your garden or bedroom, a book or on the river. If you do this work for long, you will need a vehicle that transports you from the worries at work.

# Ethical Treatment

SKEPTICAL READERS MAY WONDER WHY WE HAVEN'T BROUGHT UP THE subject of journalistic ethics until chapter twelve. After all, ethics are a daily consideration in every TV newsroom. For our purposes, it makes better sense to put it after our discussion of how we work. And everything can't go in order of importance. "Stairway to Heaven" is the <u>fourth</u> track on Led Zeppelin IV. That said, ethical treatment of subjects and story details is extremely important in our job.

## In the Field

Here's a short list of rules that govern ethics in the field. These are not the only rules. Rather, they are the top five. Considering them regularly will set students on the right path and keep professionals out of the boss's office.

1. *Report the facts and document events.* This is basic. One of the first things you should learn in school. And one of the first rules to apply at work. We are paid observers, not interpreters. Of course, your style and experience may color your account of a situation to some extent. Still, gather and report information as accurately as possible. Don't

change the story. When you stick with the facts, and inject human emotion as you find it, you offer an accurate, powerful account. Clearly, there are different ways to tell a single story; different angles to take and points of view to stress. Someone has to decide what's important in a story. Ultimately that person is you and your partner. In that process, you are responsible for making wise, even decisions that shape the story fairly.

2. *Elicit the sound you want with questions.* Never tell a subject what to say, ever. Ask good questions. If you are interested in a certain area of the subject matter, ask questions about it. Your job is to elicit the best sound: sound that tells the story succinctly enough for TV news, conveying human emotion.

3. *Don't move objects.* Even to get a better shot. Don't place things for dramatic or any other effect. That means you should not push a swing or hanging plant because it lends some movement to the shot. Movement helps a static shot, but journalists moving objects for effect is a mistake.

4. *Don't manufacture news.* The bottom line is we are not in the business of inventing news to make our job easier, or making it up to create a better story. Report and document, and do it as creatively as possible. But if something doesn't feel right, don't do it. Red flags go up for a reason. When they do, pay attention, ask questions, and get advice from others before going forward. (For an example of manufactured news, refer to the next chapter. Cartoonist Mark Plut swears this is a true story!)

5. *Don't accept cash or gifts to do stories.* The station pays you, not the people involved in the story you are covering. There is some grey area within this rule, but the bottom line is to remain objective. For example, I got a half a pound of coffee while doing a story about a local coffee roaster. I didn't get it as payment for doing the story. It was a small

token offered as we did a non-controversial feature story. The photographer accepted one, too. It would have been rude to say no, and accepting didn't cloud our judgment or provide them favoritism. The same could be said for the occasional hot dog, carnival ride or theatre ticket, sometimes offered to station personnel as a way to create a buzz, but not necessarily connected to a specific story. Our company policy is to deny any gifts that affect coverage or are worth more than fifty dollars.

## When to Err on the Side of Compassion—or Not

The News is fascinated with death and in a variety of unenviable settings, we deal with regular folks experiencing the worst day of their lives. We, as journalists, position ourselves to the side but as near the event as possible. This can be an uncomfortable place. Particularly, when no one wants you around or wants to talk to you or is too upset to speak on the worst day of their life. In these situations, a conscience comes in handy and feeling what it's like to wear someone else's moccasins.

No one wants to bother a grieving parent. A seventeen year old girl from the fruit orchards in Parkdale near Mt. Hood died as a passenger street racing in Portland. For a parent, it can't get much worse. I drew this assignment alone, without a reporter, which makes it more difficult. The parents were expecting me, which helped a little. Loading my gear, I told my friend, engineer Mark Sutton where I was headed and he advised I just treat them the way I would want to be treated were I in the same position. Mark knows what he's talking about. He lost a son in the Navy. So I took his advice and prepared to do the best I could.

Driving to their little farm, I mustered some resolve for this unenviable task. The exhausted parents welcomed me at the door, brought me inside and told me all about it. She was a good girl, never much trouble. The boy who was driving and survived the crash was her boyfriend. The parents knew him and had liked him. They didn't know about the street racing. Had they known, they said they would have forbid it. They wanted everyone to know that street racing was too dangerous. Then they showed me photographs of their daughter. Being able to warn other kids and parents away from this deadly recreation gave the deceased girl's parents some solace, or so it seemed at the time. They said they were glad to be able to get the word out and that perhaps some good might come from their tragedy. On the worst day of their lives, they were hoping to warn other families to avoid a misery like theirs.

Understandably, a lot of people experiencing the worst day of their life don't wish to speak to the media. There's really not much to be gained from pushing these poor people. Momentarily, you may get a sound bite. But these stories are quickly forgotten, while the family is left with pain and loss. Journalists should not inject more sting into that situation to get a dramatic sound bite or picture of grief. It gives us all a bad name.

Sometimes the toughest assignments end up being very rewarding, when you encounter grieving people who want an outlet to express themselves. It happens more often than you might imagine. Most people, by nature, want to communicate. If people are hurting, some shut down, but others want to talk. It helps them make sense of whatever the trouble is or create a positive message out of their loss. Sometimes, it elevates the deceased when family speaks out against an injustice.

Take extra care here. Treat hurting people sensitively, and tell their story the best you can. These human faces and emotions connect with viewers, make them care and make them cry. Telling these stories respectfully and well is a privilege.

For those not interested in telling their story through the local TV news, demonstrate your interest. Then leave them alone. Don't be pushy. They may want to talk tomorrow.

## Thurston

I saw the network media descend on Springfield, Oregon the day Kip Kinkel shot his parents in their home and then Ben Walker and Michael Nickelausen in the cafeteria of Thurston High School. It was a big national story. The killer was an unassuming adolescent/teenager who appeared incapable of anything more violent than pimple squeezing. The violence of his acts that day, patricide and matricide, did not match his frightened mug shot photo. How such a deep well of hate could have been dug in a seemingly nice family gave the story added value. It whipped the assembling media into a frenzy for information about the boy and his short history. Reporters, producers and photographers from around the northwest, and all the network people pushed parents around to get their stories as soon as they arrived. They also tried sneaking into churches and other areas off-limits to media in a scramble to interview grieving students. Scurrying around, trying to beat their competition, these big city journalists irritated a lot of small-towners and made a few enemies, too. An out of control media swarm that knows it's only here for the short term is the definition of a. f. u. in the news world.

The local Eugene stations had to hold back a little because these were our neighbors. We knew we were going to be living with them after this tragic story subsided. Still, we all got a black eye from the overzealous reporting and unsympathetic treatment of frightened, grieving families.

Sometimes grieving families are open to probing questions. You know when they are and when they are not. Professionals respect the latter condition. Sometimes it's best to save the hardest questions not for the grief stricken in their lowest moment, but rather for P. I. O. or family spokesperson.

In our local reporting, it would be nice to say we rose above the hue and cry of a swarming national media but unfortunately we added to it in our way. Our live trucks added to circus atmosphere just a few feet outside the school fence. We led our news cast with the story in every show for more than a month. We did little to confront the panic and fear many of our neighbor's felt. We really made it worse by reporting incessantly the same details of the mass murder, spun fresh into new stories every day. But there is another way.

In these special circumstances, stories researched and understood through a filter of compassion can be as powerful. And letting go of grim facts instead of including them in every story can give a new story freshness and an opportunity for insight.

Even in difficult situations, TV news reporters and photographers have to be prepared to ask hard questions. For these stories, it's our job to show bad people doing bad things. Susan Smith claimed a man abducted her baby. A few days later, it was discovered she had drowned the baby herself and then lied about it. Unfortunately, liars and sociopaths frequently make the news. You have to go on a case by case basis. You can't treat every grieving mother like Susan Smith. If something doesn't look right or you believe someone is lying then you have to ask that. That's what Public Information Officer's and spokespeople are for. It's your job to ask questions local citizens not present would ask or are thinking.

## Throw Back the Little Ones. Pan Fry the Big Ones.

Don't forget what it feels like to get fired. Employees sometimes talk to reporters and photographers while they are on the job. When their bosses find out and disagree with what's said or don't think it reflects well on the business, those workers can get in trouble and occasionally get fired.

Sometimes the employee is doing something he or she shouldn't. We catch them and they get fired. That's fair. Sometimes an employee wants to blow the whistle on the boss. That's fair, too. And sometimes the employee sticks up for the boss who's doing something wrong and they both get implicated. That's just tough for both of them. But the small fry who really don't have anything to say but might say something wrong and anger their boss. Leave them alone.

I forget the story. But some chucklehead popped off in an interview to get on TV. It was obvious. Gave us a good sound bite, but showing off more than reacting to the question or situation. He came off looking like, umm, what he was. The N. D. decided immediately to bag the interview, however compelling and slightly amusing, to save this guy from looking like a dork. That is not our job—to rescue the shallow end of the gene pool from themselves. Still, there's nothing wrong with throwing back the little 'fellers when the story does not require them.

## Be the Curmudgeon

Reporters are paid to ask difficult questions. Photojournalists are expected to gather pictures and sound from events while participants are telling you to leave. It's the germ of many good stories. Something happened about which the main players may not be comfortable. That's your story. What they have to say about it after the fact is your sound. Do you have video of the event from which the players are retreating? If so, you may have a good story.

In the early stages of Portland's mayoral race in 2007, back room whispers grew into accusations that the front runner, Sam Adams, had an affair with a seventeen year old from Salem. That Sam was fairly beloved by the electorate made the recrimination hard to fathom. Sam is a gay man. The seventeen year old boy he was alleged to have fondled also described himself as gay and the accuser, a local developer and second tier mayoral candidate, Bob Ball, was gay, too. The situation was confusing. Many of the people reporting on it were uncomfortable about the allegation and nature of the participants. Most of the local media preferred to distance themselves as soon as the story allowed.

Adams's political allies called it a smear. Mr. Ball said that if

Sam Adams had relations with a minor, he was not fit for public office. Sam Adams made a few recriminations of his own. And that is where the story ended for over a year. We in the media lost interest and Sam won in a landslide.

The story would have ended there were it not for one curmudgeonly print reporter, Nigel Jaquiss. In his astonishing piece for Willamette Week, Mr. Jaquiss named the teenage boy, now a nineteen year old, Beau Breedlove. A name to fit his new-found fame. Within a few days, the mayor's office was in full damage control. A press conference was called and everyone who had given Sam the benefit of the doubt or was just too busy to run down the facts was there to pounce. Such contrition. Never were the words "sorry" and "mistake" uttered more often by a big city mayor. It was true, Sam and Beau had a relationship when Beau was just seventeen. Was it consensual? Yes. Did they have sex? We'll never know. There is a re-call effort underway which may not get much traction. This drama might have been avoided had we journalists pushed a little harder for the facts behind the original accusation. This would have saved the electorate some consternation, too.

Asking uncomfortable questions does not make you popular. It may convince media critics of their own worst suspicions about our character and motives. But it is our job. To ask the questions a citizen, viewer or curiosity seeker is asking in their head.

Not every story requires a curmudgeon. It is our job to ask tough questions no one is comfortable asking. But with some stories, there is no dark underbelly that needs turning over. If it's a story about a man and his dog, do you need to ask if he stole the dog?

Much of the time, there is no conspiracy. All you need are good questions that prompt telling answers. This leads to brisk story telling. I am all about asking probing questions when warranted, and I agree reporters don't always do that. Be tough when the story calls for it, otherwise be cool.

## No Such Thing as "Off the Record"

Frequently, we hear from professional public information officers, "I'll tell you something *off the record. . .*"

What does that mean? The implication is that it's information you can know but not repeat in your story. Or it may mean that you can repeat the information without naming the source. In either case, the informant trusts you to do something unstated.

If a source tells you something off the record which you can corroborate, you should be able to use that information in spite of their ideas about giving such information off the record. I think people who like to give information off the record have watched "All the President's Men" too many times. As professionals, they should know any information which double checks as truthful can be used to tell your story.

It is fair to remind this person that everything they say will be checked out and possibly included in the story. Then again, they might hold back that juicy morsel of information they only want to divulge off the record. In any case, do not name them as your source.

Use caution with off the record conversations and information. If you can confirm what's been told to you off the record, you can go with it. I would only name the confirming source. Often, off the record information is a starting point, and requires some digging to build confirmation, and get the story on the air. You could "out" your off the record source, but it will probably be the last time they trust you. On the other hand, if you can get the information out there without naming the off the record source, that may be what they hoped would happen. And they may feed you inside information again for other stories in the future.

# Are News People Vultures?

After a live shot at Emmanuel Hospital in northeast Portland, I was bent over, reeling in cable. A nurse walked by me and in a conversational tone remarked on our efforts there that afternoon.

"Vultures."

Ouch. And I thought we'd been doing a pretty good job up until then. Apparently, everyone didn't think so. In the moment, I really felt like telling this lady to shove it. I'd just worked a long day, perhaps not unlike herself. But I let the comment pass and finished reeling in the cable, still smarting from the barb.

I've looked back on that episode many times to understand why she said what she said, and to what degree that anonymous nurse was correct in her judgment of me and this business as she observed it that afternoon.

She might have given some thought to why we in the news business seem obsessed with death. First off, there isn't a busy news room in the country where the question isn't asked occasionally,

"Did anyone die?"

Just a few weeks ago, a producer in a fit of frustration blurted out, "Is that guy gonna kill himself or what?"

In most other moments, that producer is a kind, sensitive girl. Mother of a couple of kids. Not the type to wish strangers would hurry up and kill themselves.

Yeah, news rooms are very interested whenever people die. Mortality is important, critical to many story's importance. It's not the only thing or the most important thing. It isn't necessarily the most interesting thing. But if someone dies in an accidental, intentional or natural way, it can be important. People want to know why, how, when and where. It's human nature. Not the most flattering part of it, but natural. Perhaps we are rationalizing bad behavior.

Critics of our business, like the nurse, might argue that TV news has too many stories about death. In presenting so many stories where death is an element, we pander to and celebrate the lowest common denominator. We revel in a viewer's worst instincts. By presenting it in bite size pieces, we encourage it. This begets more murder, crime and everything else that's bad in society.

TV news holds up a mirror to the cities we work in. Sometimes the reflection isn't pretty. It's ugly how some people treat each other. And easy to condemn the bearer of that message.

I think to be fair, were I that nurse, I would remind news people that when people die at an accident scene and helicopters orbit above the wreckage and ambulances, we resemble vultures. Plainly. That's hard to argue with. And when she drives by the flashing lights and ambulances on the freeway, does she turn to look? What is she looking for? Isn't that human nature—to be interested in catastrophe? Why is the long-running show "Cops" popular? We are fascinated by the shirtless dude sitting on the curb lying to a cop. The news on television gives us a window into people and their stories we don't encounter normally. Would we be better off if we ignored it?

We are vultures at times, when you have to try to get an interview with the wife of the husband who got hit by the car, the parents of the child that died, or the wife of the solider killed in Iraq. It goes with the territory we cover, unfortunately. It is a tough part of the job, getting that painful story of human loss. I'd rather do a story with real people in it than the city council meeting. So it becomes about how you do it. Do you have genuine empathy for the people you are approaching, and do you treat them fairly? Does the story do them justice? Are you representing their feelings in a way they will appreciate and you can feel good about? Are you telling the truth, and at the same time telling it with the real emotion these people have provided for your story? It can be a powerful and humbling experience to meet people in pain, and tell their story. Do it right and you can feel proud of your effort.

On occasion, what we do or are asked to do it is just wrong. A little girl was the victim of sex abuse in a local clothing store. A man was exposing himself to the six year old (and touching himself), while the mother was trying on shoes. The mom didn't see it happening, and the man did it repeatedly while the child sat an just an aisle away from her. It was all caught on a surveillance camera. We ran the story live in the afternoon, which I presented from the scene. The Sheriff's office was handling it, and the Public Information Officer was very helpful getting us details and the in-store video, which we used judiciously. *He also told me the family of the girl did not wish to be contacted for the story. He had already checked with them.* I was working a late shift, and was told to advance the story (find a new angle) for the eleven o'clock news. My bosses insisted I figure out where the little girl lived and ask the family to talk to us. I was livid. We were dealing with a PIO that knew what he was doing. He had a history of getting us everything he could and doing it right. I had to call him back and ask for the family's contact information, or an investigative report that would provide it. Now he was livid. He said, "I told you they do not want contact." I told him my bosses were making me try to do it anyway. He reminded me in a forceful way that the case involved a child sex abuse victim.

"There's no way in hell I'm giving your station their personal contact information. We don't indentify sex abuse victims of any age."

My bosses insisted the mother might be persuaded to be interviewed (maybe in silhouette) to express her anger at the incident. Our efforts caused the PIO to call my News Director directly and give her a piece of his mind. I'm glad he did.

## NPPA Ethics Guidelines

These rules were handed out at the National Press Photographer's Workshop in 2001. Hard to find one word worth changing. We repeat them with permission, please.

# Ethics Code

1. Photojournalists and those who manage visual news productions are accountable for upholding the following standards in their daily work:
2. Be accurate and comprehensive in the representation of subjects.
3. Resist being manipulated by staged photo opportunities.
4. Be complete and provide context when photographing or recording subjects. Avoid stereotyping individuals and groups. Recognize and work to avoid presenting one's own biases in the work.
5. Treat all subjects with respect and dignity. Give special consideration to vulnerable subjects and compassion to victims of crime or tragedy. Intrude on private moments of grief only when the public has an overriding and justifiable need to see.
6. While photographing subjects do not intentionally contribute to, alter, or seek to alter or influence events.
7. Editing should maintain the integrity of the photographic image's content and context. Do not manipulate images or add or alter sound in any way that can mislead viewers or misrepresent subjects.
8. Do not pay sources or subjects or reward them materially for information or participation.
9. Do not accept gifts, favors, or compensation from those who might seek to influence coverage.
10. Do not intentionally sabotage the efforts of other journalists.

Outside ethical considerations, the NPPA has these recommendation for photojournalists.

1. Strive to ensure that the public's business is conducted in public. Defend the rights of access for all journalists.
2. Think proactively, as a student of psychology, sociology,

politics and art to develop a unique vision and presentation. Work with a voracious appetite for current events and contemporary visual media.

3. Strive for total and unrestricted access to subjects, recommend alternatives to shallow or rushed opportunities, seek a diversity of viewpoints, and work to show unpopular or unnoticed points of view.

4. Avoid political, civic and business involvements or other employment that compromise or give the appearance of compromising one's own journalistic independence.

5. Strive to be unobtrusive and humble in dealing with subjects.

6. Respect the integrity of the photographic moment.

7. Strive by example and influence to maintain the spirit and high standards expressed in this code. When confronted with situations in which the proper action is not clear, seek the counsel of those who exhibit the highest standards of the profession.

8. Photojournalists should continuously study their craft and the ethics that guide it.

## Phoners

The vast majority of telephone interviews whose audio airs on the news are conducted and recorded in the newsroom. Most phoners happen between reporters and public officials giving information. The conversation airs with a graphic of the person's name and their agency/affiliation. It is almost always the case that these interview subjects know their conversation is being recorded because the interviewer says so up front. This is called "two party consent". It is a legal requirement in most states. Where this law applies, you cannot record a conversation and then air or print its contents without consent of both parties. To do so would be unethical and could land one in legal trouble.

Some states have single party consent. Like the phrase implies, the interviewer is not legally required to inform the interviewee the call is being recorded. Even in these circumstances, ethical journalistic considerations come into play. Is the interview subject confiding in you, the reporter, because you've given her the impression that you aren't using the interview information in your story? Then you've tricked the subject into divulging something. That sort of information gathering is unethical. Responsible journalists are up front about their intentions. You should never mislead someone on the phone or anywhere to get information or video.

# Anatomy of Your Typical News Story

Stinky Teriyaki—A True Story

# Professional Etiquette

## Funerals

We are frequently invited to funerals. These can be private or, as in the case of a soldier who has fallen in the line of duty, a public event. For the latter, there are public officials and politicians present. Like a press conference, these public people are usually available for interviews.

Families of a fallen soldier should be approached first through a spokesperson or P. I. O. Use common sense. It's impolite and disrespectful to fire questions at the family of the deceased even at public events, unless they approach you or their representative says they're available.

Protocol at private funerals is tricky. We don't pretend to be writing the rules here. Every funeral is different, so you have to think on your feet. Often, rules for the media will be laid out before you arrive. Like this:

"The family would like you all to sit in the balcony. They won't be making any statements."

There are many news gathering situations where we don't follow any instructions and should not have to. A funeral is not one of those. If there is one hard and fast rule for reporting on funerals, it is to follow the family's instructions. Do not intrude where you are not wanted. Be respectful.

Do not be late and dress appropriately. You would not believe the attire people wear to funerals these days. Team jackets! Shorts! Professional media should rise above that sort of display. You may be able to make a good impression on the family you wish to speak with and get an interview by being respectful and following protocol. Good manners count at funerals. When the media demonstrates appropriate restraint, we get thrown a bone or two.

## Strategy

While reporters are usually welcome, often just a single photographer is sent to gather video of the funeral for all present TV media. One camera is less obtrusive and distracting. This is a pool cam situation, like we described in the earlier section. The funeral pool cam exercise though, is not so brief as inside a court room therefore it behooves one to limit himself. A funeral service can last over an hour. If you roll on everything, there will be too much tape to log. You're doing your colleagues a disservice by over-shooting. Be ready to roll on the most emotional speeches, skip the boring stuff, get some music, every good sequence, some cutaways and don't forget to show the family. This last element is sometimes difficult to gather, but you will need a shot of the family for every funeral story, even if it's gathered from the balcony.

Record all the elements you'll need for your story, but avoid over-shooting. Shoot the amount and variety of shots you would need to fashion an interesting, informative package of the event. For the sake of your colleagues who'll have to shape a story with unfamiliar pictures and sound, don't hand them ninety minutes of tape. They will cringe.

## Courtrooms

There should be only a minimum of talking between you and your reporter if you are shooting inside a courtroom during a trial. Better to have a few hand signals, so you know when not to roll. Be careful not to move around too much or create a distraction, especially if you have to break down your gear and leave before court is finished for the day.

Most people working inside the courtroom turn off cell phones or set them to pulse. I did this one day in court in Marion County. We were not the pool camera, so I sat in to observe the trial of man accused of setting a house fire that killed two people.

In the middle of things, my phone vibrated at my belt, but I did not answer it. Only a few minutes later, the phone actually rang aloud in court. I was horrified. It couldn't be my phone. I'd set it to vibrate. But it was my phone. There was some crazy default that made it ring if someone left a voice mail.

The judge looked squarely at me and told me to leave immediately. She also instructed the bailiff to confiscate my phone. I saw the defendant looking straight at me with a disgusted look. He was later convicted of arson and manslaughter, eventually receiving a long sentence in state prison. The lessons I took from this very unprofessional moment were two fold. If an arsonist gives you a look that says you lack appropriate respect for the legal system, even though he's an arsonist he still might be correct. And just turn off the cell phone before you walk into court.

## Friendly Adversaries: How to Deal With Police

The relationship between the media and police alternates between friendly and adversarial. We have a job to do: telling truthful, compelling stories about subjects the public has a right to know. Law enforcement agencies have to balance the public's right to information with doing strong investigations that result in convictions. Add to this balance the weight of political pressure by the city or state to do no wrong and not cover up. The media watches the scale tip back and forth knowing citizens expect accountability from public agencies, especially police. In the long run, police, troopers and marshals with a sophisticated understanding of the "friendly adversary" nature of our relationship know transparency is the best course.

Your relationship with the police can be a fine relationship, and it can be productive. But you often must rely on the Police Department's willingness to talk to you to get the story. Some agencies are more willing to work with you, while others ARE NOT.

Cops have a tough job. I wouldn't want to be one. I respect and admire most officers very much. But you have to hold police accountable. It means extra work. You can't always take what they feed you. Sometimes, you have to look for the other story. You obviously want the police side of it, and for the most part you will get cooperation. Good information from police officials usually stems from an effort by departments seeking greater transparency.

But it really matters with whom you are dealing. Earlier in the year, I covered an officer involved shooting in Marion County. A city policeman shot a twenty year old man to death during a burglary. The district attorney wouldn't allow the police department to release anything. All we knew was that an officer shot a man. It occurred in the street near a home that was the address of a "burglary in progress" call to the county. The only information we were given were some names and the time police were dispatched.

We did the best we could under the circumstances. We had to do the dance we do, waiting for the police to release information. In the meantime, we talked to several friends of the young man who was shot. They all agreed he was great kid, and never in trouble. Indeed, he had no police record. As it turned out, the young man, high on drugs, was coming at police with a broken beer bottle. The grand jury exonerated the officer involved.

With everyday crime stories, more than physical barricades may go up. Street cops can be gruff and unhelpful. Get to know them. Be friendly. But know your rights as a citizen and member of a free press. Don't let them push you back farther than the police line, or than the general public is allowed. Don't let them allow neighbors to come and go through police tape, and keep you back without a very good reason. And inquire professionally as to the reason. If the explanation seems flimsy or arbitrary, they need to provide a supervisor or PIO for your questions and concerns. Most cops know you have a job to do and will let you do it, as long as you don't interfere with them doing theirs.

# The Student Section

## So You Want to Go into TV News?

Students need to take a hard look before getting into this line of work. Granted, there are worse jobs and first careers for twenty-somethings, fresh out of college. Be prepared for heavy deadline pressures. It's likely newsroom managers will not be outstanding at news or managing. Those same managers may be as motivated to satisfy corporate goals as any journalistic ones. This industry is sometimes difficult to love and harder to stay in. That aside, being a reporter or photographer covering the news in your city is not boring. You will get next to some of the most interesting people and events there.

## Some Advice for Aspirants

Local TV news is where students going into this profession usually wind up working; their first job out of college will be in a small market somewhere. And even after several years in this profession, it is not likely you'll be at CNN, New York City or LA. Possible, but improbable.

Not many "J" school students I've worked with say their career goal is to be a reporter, photographer or anchor in market one hundred forty six. But local news, in small, medium and larger markets is the likeliest destination for journalism students who pursue TV news. There's nothing wrong with wanting to be the next Walter Cronkite or Christiane Amanpour. Every kid on the playground wants to be the next Michael Jordan. That's healthy and ambitious. A few will reach that position. Out of two hundred or so co-workers and colleagues at other stations I've worked with in thirteen years, one photographer, one reporter and one meteorologist have advanced to some national news venue (CNN and ABC's L.A. bureau.) It's not impossible, but there's only so much room at the tippy top.

That said, lessons learned well in your first few markets can transport you to the networks. In fact, that's the most certain vehicle for success: be a good story teller, a thorough professional and the broader TV news world will beat a path to your resume' and reel. It may sound corny, but being that photojournalist, reporter, producer or news anchor in market one forty six is an honorable profession. It's hard work which, done well, can yield a lot of satisfaction and make you happy in your work and your life.

This is not your father's news any more. Many senior reporters and photographers are getting out of the business. That is, when they're not being forced out by bosses not renewing contracts or giving raises. There is a natural attrition in every job and especially physically demanding ones like ours. But there's a pattern in markets small to large, getting away from more experienced, better paid professionals in the direction of younger, less experienced and less expensive replacements. Sometimes stations maintain ratings while going to this youth movement while cutting loose their most experienced people. This has loosened a few boulders that threaten a landslide burying another layer of older reporters. This trend of replacing experienced journalists with younger ones should be encouraging for students because more than ever, there is room to move for people entering the business.

There's also the attitude that many young women being hired as reporters receive these offers based on their looks alone. As opposed to men who are hired for their experience or journalistic skill. I offer it here because I know a lot of people who agree with it. Mostly men. I've never heard a single female colleague express it. I think the reason is because women have to work harder to compete with men in any virtually any profession, just to be considered the equal of a male co-worker (who probably earns more than she does.) So the "hottie factor" in hiring woman reporters doesn't seem like much an edge to me. And if there are a few professions in which women may have some advantage, is that unfair? Not to me. What is unfair is the glass ceiling that exists in media corporations in general. Currently, the CEO of the company I work for is a woman, which is unusual and a step in the right direction. But when you look at the boards of the very largest media corporations in the world – mostly men. Rupert Murdoch's Fox conglomerate has a board of fourteen people. One is a woman. A little lower down the food chain, fewer than a quarter of local TV news directors are women. That's why the complaint that some new reporter just got hired because of her looks sounds hollow. And hopefully not strong enough to keep the glass ceiling firmly overhead.

## Preparing for a Career

Study hard. Well-schooled journalists have an advantage, because everyone in the news room doesn't have a journalism degree. Many have a journalism degree and about an equal number have a journalism background. But this doesn't mean everyone in either group has clear ideas about what aspects of their education apply or do not apply to their everyday work.

Don't limit your study to books. Get an internship. Find something you can do inside a newsroom, like write or run a teleprompter. Do it long enough to get a feel for what it would be like to work there forty hours a week. Also, go out in the field with photographers and reporters. Experience their work. How do they like their job? Or not. Interns should remember to ask what aspects of the job we professionals like, or dislike. Then you might know if this business is for you. And have an idea of what kind of journalist you want to be.

Students who begin their internship star struck by TV reporters and anchors might need a reality check. Don't think you're going to get rich in this profession. Most of us aren't.

## The Most Interesting Job in the World

This oft-heard phrase gets pushed at the award banquets and professional conferences. It's motivating, thrown around as kind of a dare. If you can't repeat it with the requisite zeal, you probably have an attitude problem.

Still, we occasionally hear co-workers describe their work this way. But not usually when they are at work. Yesterday, a reporter invoked the phrase as he was leaving to take a job with the local fire department.

As jobs go, this one's better than most. Every day is a little different. You meet very interesting, sometimes crazy people. Your co-workers are a gas and seeing your efforts on TV between five and seven is a special gratification. In one eight hour shift, you may get the opinion of the state epidemiologist about a disease outbreak then drive half an hour to interview a remorseful father who accidentally backed over his daughter on a riding mower. You can't beat this job if you enjoy variety or people.

## Class Projects

Most TV Production classes have students producing their own stories. A good classroom project has a lot in common with successful TV news stories. Look for an interesting story in the first place. Is it visual? Are there two sides to the story? Will everyone talk? What is the story? What is interesting about the story?

For your class project, who do you know that does something

interesting? Any age. A hobby, athletic event, a group that meets to do something together. Now, you have people, action and if they like what they do, even if they struggle, you have emotion. Especially if they struggle. This would be a feature story.

For something harder and with an edge, you will need two sides that disagree. An on-campus debate is fine, but it's all sound bites and talking heads. If you can bring in video of the subject they are debating then you can put together a story that is interesting to watch and listen to.

Get familiar with your gear. Know how to white balance the camera correctly by bringing a white card or sheet of paper with you. Make sure the microphones work properly and you can listen through headphones or an ear piece as you record sound. Is the tripod steady? Tighten some screws to get rid of any wobble.

Once you clear the twin hurdles of story and gear, you can get to work.

## Don't Expect a Pat on the Back

Your typical newsroom is not a place where one should expect much acknowledgement or praise. Awards may come your way, if you're good. But this is likely as close as you'll come to praise, so don't be needy.

I don't expect much in the praise department, so I am rarely disappointed. I won a couple awards one quarter and thought someone might say something. Eventually, a manila folder appeared in my mail slot. The contents were two awards with my name on each. Turned up in one corner of the folder was some writing about an inch long. I moved in close to read it. It said, "congrats".

It may be different for network people. But if you need an ego stroke regularly, you'll be frustrated in local TV news. Lou Dobbs described it as "liberating" when you no longer work for or expect a big thank you at the end of the day. Then the motivation to do good work comes from inside and the satisfaction one derives from doing their job well is deeper than a pat on the back.

Don't expect much sympathy from a local TV newsroom if you're sick. Lots of people work when they're ill in news rooms because calling in sick is frowned upon. This trend spreads the sickness further. We regularly report stories during cold and flu season with medical professionals encouraging people to stay home when they feel unwell, yet we fail to follow the advice when it comes to our workplace. Frequently, people are encouraged to come in for work while they are trying to call in sick. For that reason, many unions put specific language in their contracts that member's sick days cannot be questioned.

Recently, a photographer in our shop worked on Thanksgiving when she had a contagious flu, and should have stayed in bed. She came to work though, because as she saw it, calling in sick on Thanksgiving would have been too coincidental and she would not have been believed.

## The Most Important Question We Forgot to Ask

This is frequently the last question asked in an interview. Is there something the interviewee' knows that she thinks is essential to the story that your line of questions never reached? Now that we've arrived at the end of this book, we ask the question of ourselves. Journalism students may wish to ask another question.

"Yeah, but do you like your job?"

Life has its little ups and downs, like the song says. And so does this job. When the ups last longer than the downs, you're doing well. In work or life. With a decent attitude, the good outweighs the bad in TV news. With a negative attitude or dislike of co-workers, this job hangs around your neck like a hundred pound weight. Those folks get out, if they're smart. An overnight producer quit recently and his goodbye e-mail was titled "so long, suckers". He went on to list the things he wouldn't miss about the station and took a few parting swipes at some people whose patience <u>he</u> was regularly challenging. Perhaps he should have gotten out a bit sooner.

But how many jobs really are different every day? This one is. That doesn't mean it's always a gas, gas, gas. But it's not boring. Some days, we wish it were a little bit boring.

## Getting Started

Perhaps in this ramble, we've missed one other aspect of this career that students might be most interested in.

"How does one begin a career in TV news?"

That first job. How do you get it? The short answer is: with a tape and indication of talent. Do not expect to be able to talk your way into a job—even in the smallest market. I tried it in Grand Junction, Colorado. But I've never had the charisma or persuasiveness to make that work. I had to get a tape together. In my case, it was a documentary on trout conservation. Forty five minutes long. Most students will have an easier road. Producing a tape in class or internship (see the section "Interns" in Chapter 6) can be arrived at if you're not afraid to ask for help. Everyone gets started this way, more or less. You need a tape and, of course, resume'. Neither has to be astonishingly good, just good.

It helps too, if you're flexible about where you start. Rarely do students come out of "J" School and start working as reporters or photojournalists in markets larger than 100. Look in markets 120 and smaller for a place to start. And be prepared to work there a couple of years. You may be good and move up quickly. Your learning curve may be a little shallower. I spent four years in Eugene, Oregon at my first job. I learned a lot participating as a shooter in the National Press Photographer's Association Workshop. Meeting some highly skilled photojournalists and getting to know them that week made me realize I might approach their level someday.

# For Our Colleagues

## An Approach Worth Maintaining

It doesn't matter how opulent your newsroom is nor in how large a market it's located. In fact, your newsroom may be a classroom. In all cases, your goal for each general assignment is the same. Tell the story the most accurate and compelling way. Everything else is sub-category, window dressing.

To tell your story best, take ownership. It's what you are getting paid to do. Take it. Defend it. Don't let anyone wrestle it from you because it's different from what producers or colleagues believed the story was in the morning meeting. Get into it. Personalize it in your head at the start. What do you think about it? What's interesting about this story to you? Where's the juice?

Remain interested, but objective. Balance both sides in a clear, compelling way. Do not take sides during an interview. Subjects are people, just like photographers and reporters. Understand their position and stories based on your experience. What you believe is the story, based on your hearing and seeing of it, will inform what you write and shoot. That is the personal side of journalism you cannot and should not try to get around. Impersonal stories told without much involvement from the writer or photographer are deadly boring. Unfortunately, they are fairly common, so there's plenty of room for story tellers and photojournalists who care.

Conversely, your personal opinion has little room in your final script or edited package. Remember you are recounting the details and the scene to tell a story of what happened. Use the most telling pictures and sound to make the final edited news story move. What does not matter is your view or beliefs about a story. Most viewers don't care what you think, either. They want the facts and pictures as the story happened, so they can make up their own mind about it.

It's your job to tell the story that honestly represents the people you include in the piece. These are the people whose perspective matters most, the ones that the story is about. Their feelings and opinions will shape your story. Formulate these perspectives in a logical, balanced and even colorful way. You decide what the story is about. Your initial impressions may change as you gather information, sound and pictures. So don't make up your mind in haste. Rather, let the people you meet in the process say what they think, and build the story around them. Be true to their account. Then balance what they say against your personal impressions and journalistic instincts.

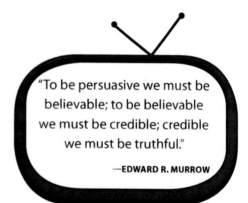

"To be persuasive we must be believable; to be believable we must be credible; credible we must be truthful."

—EDWARD R. MURROW

## Be a Damn Professional

The dynamics of getting along with your workmates is interesting and challenging. Some of my co-workers are my best friends. Others I tolerate in a professional manner. As a reporter you must be cool and collected, in the newsroom and even more so in the field. I think I'm considered by my peers to be a pretty easy going guy. But I have my moments. Hell, I have my days. It's a stressful business where people and technology collide, sometimes crash and burn. Seeing eye to eye with co-workers (and community members) and not getting on each other's nerves can be tough. There are photographers I prefer to work with, but I generally don't get to choose, nor should I. This is part of being professional: work with whomever you are paired with, whether you like them or not. Be looking down the line for a train wreck whenever reporters complain about certain photographers or vice versa, and management tries to accommodate their dislikes.

On the flip side, assignment folks may understand certain pairings work better than others, and will take advantage of that fact. . . nothing wrong with that. For the most part, TV news people are a congenial bunch, with wit and wisdom on our side and a pinch of passion sprinkled in. That passion can be a driving force that helps us in our work, but sometimes it gets us into trouble. Spirited debates are fine—personal attacks are not. Have fun with your work friends, keep it professional and don't sweat the small stuff. Your blood pressure will thank you and you'll last longer in this crazy business.

In the entire field of TV news, there is no relationship more crucial to a good news product than the working relationship between photographers and reporters. It is your collective eyes, ears, heart and intellect that viewers will see and respond to. Or not. To process the most relevant information into the most interesting, informative package, it helps to have an easy relationship with your reporter or photographer. This allows for suggestions and ideas about the story to fly around, be accepted or rejected without injuring anyone's feelings.

The most successful teams of reporters and photographers get along well and are friends outside of work. But that is not necessary to produce great stories. You need only be professional—open to the other person's ideas enough to consider them above your own.

You may find yourself working alongside someone with less experience than yourself. An easy working relationship and sharing of ideas is critical for both the experienced and inexperienced. The latter should be open to suggestions from their more experienced co-worker. Veterans should not be too bossy about what they expect.

This job of news gathering is as much about the ride as the result. Try not to become married to your own ideas, and accept another's vision for the story you share. Good journalistic collaborations involve a creative process that can take a project to a higher level. When your ideas are valued and included, you become more invested in the outcome and will work harder to make your story memorable.

## Small Victories

This is a National Press Photographers Association axiom every reporter and photographer understands, particularly during a difficult day in the field. You can't shoot an Emmy winning story every day. The vast majority of stories are warm ups for a great one. However, even the lousiest, least visual story will have something you can turn your professional skills to improving: a snappy sequence or compelling moment that elevates the piece, even temporarily.

## Make Yourself Happy

Work first for yourself. Don't think about pleasing others until you've know how you feel about the story and your effort to deliver it. Doing your work first for yourself evens out rough spots, and keeps you accountable to yourself. There will be ups and downs along your career path. They come courtesy of others who will judge what you do and how you do it. If you are like me, you won't love your job every day. But if you feel good about how hard you're working, it keeps you going—with more good days than bad. You handle the opinions of others better, knowing how you feel first. Take care of yourself, do a good job, and the rest should fall into place.

## Go with the Emotion

I appreciate Bob Heye's judgment during breaking news, and anytime. He's a seasoned reporter with a knack for knowing the layout, circumstances and stories that came before. Good writer, too. Unfortunately, this day he's limping from an achy hip. In the morning meeting, he was the oldest general assignment reporter by fifteen years. We got an afternoon "hurry up" to some smoke. Big apartment fire. Some flames and excited firemen and "lookie-loos" (Put me on TV!) Bob learned from Tualatin Valley Fire that one lady in a wheelchair was rescued early in the event. Good factoid, no follow. Plenty of good sound from excited neighbors. Public Information Officers eager to tout the department's effort. Some flamage. Matched action of a fireman putting on his hood, hiking up the ladder and arriving at the crow's nest. Driving between the fire and police cruisers, Bob saw two ladies getting out of their car. One bent over a walker.

"Just pull over. Park here."

Still bothered by his hip, Bob made his way to the ladies and after winning them over, convinced the walker-bound one to let me come in with the camera. Doreen.

"I heard a POW! Then I realized the fire was in the apartment above mine. Everything I own was in that apartment. My treadmill and TV's. I lost everything. . ."

Dissolving into sobs, this handicapped woman had few physical or economic reserves. It was hard to think about anything as she moved away one walker length at a time. Bob reminded me.

"Get some more shots of her."

I tracked this lady shuffling sadly past the engines and trucks.

Our story that evening closed with the shot of her leaving. Before the package aired Bob said he thought the ending was right.

But it is a shame when good, experienced reporters leave local TV news. Nobody benefits really. Thank goodness, Bob is still here.

But at age forty eight, he's a dinosaur. A dinosaur with the instincts to survive the freeze.

## In My Tribe

In a TV market the size of Portland, Oregon (number 22 with a bullet), there are only a few score full-time TV reporters and photographers. That means we see the same faces from the competition several times a week. Over time, they become more than faces. You know about each other's families, work situations, who they're dating and what teams they root for. We see each other at parties, work and social. So the truth of the matter is that we look out for each other. We realize that in capricious economic times, our fates are tied together. We need each other while we compete to get a greater share of the ratings; watching the backs of our colleagues, hoping they'll watch ours when stories get a little out-of-control. (Thanks, Rod, for rescuing my sticks at the "Timberline Climber Rescue" yesterday.) The local media is like a club where the requirements for membership are a powerful work ethic, sense of humor, journalistic acumen and the ability to keep your cool while the person next to you has lost his.

# Epilogue: Cherish No Illusion

OUR ORIGINAL TITLE FOR THE LAST CHAPTER WAS "DREAM WHEN You're Feeling Blue", but we wanted something more optimistic, so we plagiarized Joseph Stalin's warning to Adolph Hitler. As Russia refused to lay down for the Third Reich, neither can we accept some of the most glaring inadequacies of our business. Pilgrims have grievances. There is reason to believe in a bright future for local TV news. Here are a few suggestions for improving what we do while attracting viewers.

**Stop live coverage of school shootings.** All the attention paid to school shootings, the live pictures, excited journalists elaborating on those images, fans the flame of sociopathic behavior in susceptible teenagers and increases the likelihood of a copycat scenario. Every expert on the subject cites media attention and fame as one of the principal motivators for teenage boys who bring guns to school with the intention of perpetrating a mass killing. It is frequently cited as the main reason for some of these terrible events. Many school shooters admit to a desire to achieve fame through the act of killing at school. The Columbine shooters, Harris and Klebold, wanted to become cult heroes and shed their loser status by taking revenge against their schoolmates. The same could be said for Kip Kinkel. It's a sad reality that when this fame arrives, the killer is more important than the people he killed. A responsible media would deny them this and take away these twisted, teenage boys dreams of martyrdom and notorious fame. Removing one of the largest motivations for these acts of violence against children would likely reduce their occurrence.

**Return to stories with a public service message.** These stories generally do not produce the kind of ratings station owners crave. But everyone at the top is making enough money that they can afford to kick down a few crumbs in the name of public service. This was one of the original aims of television: improving the community we live in by disseminating important public information. Now, the news is too often glorified entertainment with little message or conscience. It exists solely to keep viewers watching.

"What's wrong with that? If you don't like it, turn it off!"

We are saying, we could be more civic-minded without crashing and burning financially. We could earn back some of the respect our industry has lost in recent years and provide a benefit for viewers. We should strive to report subjects more lofty than fatal car accidents. No one gains much from that sort of story.

One way we might generate news that's motivated by public service as much as profit is returning to the fifteen and thirty minute "Special Reports". Dig deeply into the most interesting, important stories of the day. These don't have to be dry documentary, but rather newspaper stories with good visual elements. That means the sawmill shutting down in Roseburg. The last day of music class before the district cuts the curriculum. Many interesting, important, visual stories with broad impact deserve longer treatment than a minute and a half.

**Stop doing stories about kooky celebrities and calling it news.** If you've got to talk about it, do a "celebrity gossip" segment. But don't blend it with news stories. It just diminishes everything that comes after. Remember the CNN anchor who refused to read a story about some underdressed pop tart that got scorched? This should be the exclusive realm of the "Hollywood Insider" shows which can wallow in this nonsense.

Sometimes it is fun. Everyone occasionally reads Hollywood gossip or watches a show devoted to this entertainment "news". But that's where this superficial stuff belongs. Not on local TV news. There's no evidence it boosts ratings. Most professional journalists are embarrassed reading it.

During the heyday of local TV news, when a greater percentage of eyes watched their local stations for news, there was no celebrity gossip at all.

**No more suicides as news.** Most news rooms say they avoid doing any suicide stories. But if there's some aspect of the story that's interesting, then newsrooms frequently go ahead with the story and play down the suicidal tendencies of the subject. We forget our policy when it's convenient or we're just desperate to fill time.

**Skip the school bomb scares.** Some selfish, confused kids enjoy calling in fake bomb threats to close their school for the day. They watch the building lock down, classmates sent home, and then enjoy the coverage local TV news usually gives the incident. Getting played by a sixteen year old with anger issues makes everyone look bad. If there's no real angle to the story other than inconvenienced parents or evacuated students then we should skip it. Let schools handle this mess without interference.

A genuine bomb threat is news. But we should resist sending crews and dispatching helicopters until a bomb is confirmed.

**Stop scaring viewers to get them to watch.**

"And coming up. Why the deadly swine flu may already be in Oregon. And what you can do to avoid it."

Too often, writers and producers use fear to motivate people to watch or just stay tuned through the break. Then when the story comes around, it's usually not as dire as the tease implies. The point is, we scare or worry viewers into staying around through the break.

This device is a bad practice. In the first place, you don't really deliver what you promised. You've got to make good on all those little promises in the tease. When you can't, viewers realize they've been tricked and change the channel anyway. It's disingenuous, untruthful and reinforces the perception that news paints the world negatively. Not to put too fine a point on it, but if something genuinely bad is coming to a neighborhood near you, stick to the facts. Do not monger fear for rating's sake.

**Keep live trucks well away from houses and people whose family recently died.** How would you feel if a family member died in some untimely way and shortly thereafter you saw live trucks outside your home? If the deceased was doing something nefarious or is a public person, that may change the strategy. But for ordinary people who had someone in their family die tragically, we need to show respect for the family and keep our noisy, bright live trucks away from their home. In the case of the Thurston High School shootings, students later complained the live trucks outside school added an extra element of trauma to a horrific morning. The trucks outside the school in the following few days and weeks stirred their recollection of that day.

**Eliminate live shots that don't add anything.** Superfluous live shots impede our ability to get the story. Producers and managers tell us the research shows viewers want to see us "out in the community", "on the scene", etc. These same viewers turn off their TV's and turn away from the banality of a reporter standing in front of a building where something happened three hours ago. Quit wasting the viewer's time with live shots that don't add to the story.

**Give your people constructive feedback and training.** Send them to a workshop or professional conference. Bring in a Bob Dotson or the like, to teach a day's lesson. This is one of those expendables that seem to be getting the axe at most stations, and it's too bad. Monty and I will never forget the day we had Wayne Freedman come and visit us at our little station in Eugene many moons ago. A little full of himself that day, Wayne was enlightening and funny. And I learned things. That's what it is all about: *getting better as you go.* Stations at all levels should invest in teaching, NPPA for photographers, Poynter Institute for reporters. And let's not forget our managers. It's clear most have had no training in how to manage people. Get those Assignment Managers, EP's, Managing Editors and News Directors to some training classes where they might learn the fundamentals of successful leadership. It seldom comes naturally.

**Pay people fairly.** What an outrageous idea! There is still plenty of money to go around in television, despite the goals of stockholders and hedge fund operators. Who's more important to the operation? Your employees who are giving their working lives to your business? Or stock holders, many of whom are unaware that they have stock in your company. Take some of those profits and pay your people what they are worth. Station owners should be mindful that satisfied employees are more productive.

**Pay Interns Something.** Like minimum wage for a start. Expecting a future college graduate to write vosots, pull cable for live shots or just ride around with crews in the field for free is presumptuous, cheap and, frankly, embarrassing. Managers in charge of these programs, which exist at virtually every TV station, should arrange payment of some kind for these twenty year olds with hopes of a professional journalism career. Journalism schools should insist on some payment for students who intern. Producing any aspect of your news on the backs of unpaid interns because it enhances slightly your bottom line is more bad business. Not to mention taking advantage of a group who can't really complain. News directors who practice consider interns "free help" are exploiting a group they may someday need. It doesn't have to be much, but enough to be fair.

**Wait until polls close to declare election results.** Competing amongst ourselves to declare election winners before the polls close discourages late voters. This skews results and throws a wrench into the spokes of democracy. Viewers don't care which news outlet calls a political race first. Who has six televisions tuned to six different channels anyway? Newsrooms. We subvert the voting process to earn a title no one cares about except us. It is ironic that a group with Constitutionally-protected freedoms would try to justify a self-serving game that inhibits voting. This is an example of the beast eating its own tail.

We don't always predict winners very accurately either. A few major news outlets embarrassed themselves in the 2004 Presidential election declaring winners in some states based on exit polls that proved inaccurate.

National Public Radio has a policy of not declaring winners until polls close. In the 2008 Presidential election, ABC's Charlie Gibson repeated numerous times, they would not predict a winner until "all the polls have closed." And they did not. Of course, the contest was not close and after Barack Obama won Pennsylvania's electoral votes, victory was assured. The declaration of waiting until polls close to announce a winner lifted ABC temporarily to a journalistic high ground. Were the race tighter, the networks might have reverted to form and competed to predict a winner first.

**Be a positive force for change.** Whining will get you nowhere. But if you have constructive suggestions of how to make a dysfunctional situation functional, it is your right and duty to speak up. The collaborative effort starts with good ideas about how we can better do our jobs. Speak up and stay positive.

**Keep sales and news separate**. Businesses who advertise on television then get in trouble with the law frequently get a pass from TV news operations. There's nothing wrong with stations giving advertisers special considerations. But not inside the news operation. Sales people have been known to review scripts before a story airs for content that might prove embarrassing or damage the relationship with an advertiser. News directors should put a foot down. Newsrooms should investigate any story they deem worthy without weighing it against a possible loss of advertising revenue.

**Sharing resources makes news generic and destroys competition**. There's a beast creeping toward the world of thoughtful, local TV news, good local TV news that is done well and appreciated by viewers. Its entrance is insidious and cloaked in apparent logic. Several stations employ one helicopter to cover a single story. This makes sense in markets like Los Angeles or New York where eight helicopters orbiting over a scene or following a police chase would be dangerous. But this strategy has been applied to other news situations where safety isn't a consideration.

In larger markets and stations where cost cutting is a news goal, the trend is to send one live truck to cover one story for several news outlets. It's difficult to track exactly which stations and markets are sharing news and presenting it as their own. Perhaps stations don't want to disclose the sharing of news because they're embarrassed they aren't independent of the competition. Phoenix is one market where pictures and sound are shared then aired as something exclusive, or at least produced individually.

News sharing works this way. The story gets beamed back to one receiver then travels down the fiber to other stations gathering news this way. Every station owns it at once. The exact same story. And how does it look when it airs? Almost exactly the same. The video may be edited in a different order and the script may put similar words in different places, but the stories are virtually indistinguishable.

Admittedly, many stories gathered independently wind up looking similar when they air. This is usually because economic and daily time constraints keep reporters and photojournalists from producing stories that stand out. News sharing surrenders to this limitation and institutionally concedes that a story cannot be produced in an interesting, singular fashion. Thus begins the steady march of nearly identical newscasts being broadcast simultaneously in the same market. This slouching beast may arrive before we realize it, advancing toward the warm, TV glow of competitive journalism.

Radio has been sucked into the inexorable cost-cutting and sacking of reporters; unfortunately teaming with TV stations to accomplish it. At a trial today in Salem, where a father and son were accused of planting a bomb that killed two policemen, a jury recommended that each be sentenced to death. This is the first time in thirty years a jury has expressed that in Oregon. As soon as the verdicts were read, the media scrambled out the courtroom doors to file their reports. And from the scrum of media assembled outside Marion County Courthouse, who do you think called in the 30 second "headline reports" to the Portland radio stations? The TV reporters. This, even though radio reporters sat in the same packed courtroom, elbow to elbow with the TV people. Crazy? Why would a radio station pay their own people to attend a trial, then have a TV reporter phone in <u>their</u> account? The several radio reporters agreed (as did eight other paper and TV journalists engaged in the conversation) that their job could be eliminated and perhaps soon. The radio people admitted they had been job searching outside of radio, but in the down economy of 2010 had found it difficult. So, the Beast can reach between the bars of its cage and claim victims outside. And, by the way, TV reporters doing double duty for the radio stations are not being paid for it. The radio stations are not paying them, at least so far. Managers at the TV stations have explained it's part of a reporter's assigned duties to provide the radio content. It would be reasonable to assume that radio stations are paying the TV station they are teamed with for this service. For the latter, it's a new source of revenue without much, if any, overhead. That's the beauty of it.

Consumers assume news stations compete against each other to produce the best local news. When we stop doing it the old fashioned way and viewers realize we are no longer trying to differentiate ourselves and our news product, these news consumers will look for a better product. The only way to keep the beast outside the gate of good local TV news is for stations to pursue stories independently of each other, competing to give the best coverage. By doing the best, most original work possible, we provide better coverage and give viewers a choice.

# News Room Vocabulary

**a. f. u.:** Acronym abbreviating the phrase and situation of being "all f***ed up". Pronounced ay-foo. Derived from a World War Two acronym, s.n.a.f.u., the first two letters of which stand for "situation normal."

**A-roll:** The sound of interview subjects or voice track in a story.

**B-roll:** The video and natural sound under the a-roll.

**Bite:** Sound bite, interview sound.

**Bokeh:** A still photography term for the out-of-focus portion of the frame that surrounds the focused subject.

**Butted Sound Bites:** Two sound bites in a row.

**Chutzpah (pronounced huts-pah'):** The definition of chutzpah is a man who murders his mother and father then throws himself on the mercy of the judge because he's a poor orphan. The television news business is rife with people who possess this annoying trait.

**Coaxial Cable:** The cable that brings video from your camera to whatever will receive and transmit that video signal (i. e. live truck, live studio set up, monitors etc.)

**Cold Open:** The little voiced segment at the top of the show teasing several big stories followed by swirling, whooshing graphics then the show starts.

**Cutaway:** A two shot or wide shot of the interview or press conference. Used for editing between two pieces of sound that otherwise would produce a video jump cut.

**Dichroic Filter:** Commonly refers to the mirror/filter attached the camera's battery light. The wiki definition is "a very accurate color filter used to selectively pass light of a small range of colors while reflecting other colors."

**Doubler:** The camera's telephoto switch allows you to see subjects in more close up detail and increases depth of field. It doubles approximately the telephoto strength of the lens.

**Donut:** Voiced over video directly before and after a live shot. Also called a wrap-around.

**Dub:** Duplicate copy

**Enterprising a Story:** Coming up with a story on your own. The best and most interesting stories are completely original. Not newspaper stories.

**E. P.:** Executive producer.

**Feeding the Beast:** Workplace conditions that combine unrealistic expectations and an insatiable need for more.

**Gain:** The adjustment on a camera that boosts brightness and graininess.

**General Assignment:** These are the bread and butter of every photographer and reporter. The ordinary stuff that's generated from the desk or ideas in the morning meeting. It's your job to take the ordinary out of the story and make it sing. Also called "Daily Stories".

**Hot:** Any time your picture is taken live on the air.

**HMI:** The manufacturer of lights preferred for live shots.

**IFB:** The ear piece through which you hear the producer, booth and engineers when you're in the field. The acronym for "interruptible fold back".

**Kicker:** The last story of the show, usually something fluffy, literally. Animals figure often in kickers. Everyone has a little laugh and the anchors can smile as they go out.

**Lav:** Lavaliere microphone. Rhymes with suave.

**M. M. J.:** An abbreviation for multi-media journalist.

**Mark:** A reporter's mark, like a stage actor, is the exact spot they need to stand or sit for correct camera framing.

**Mini-Pac:** A minute and a half package condensed to a buck ten.

**Mix Minus:** The audio signal received through your IFB/earpiece typically during live shots where you may hear the broadcast signal, and producer's cues without the distracting sound of your own voice live.

**Moments:** Any un-improvised expression that is surprising and interesting. When these occur in the context of the story, they are the stuff of award winning pieces.

**N. D.:** News director.

**Nats:** Natural sound, like a bird warbling or protester shouting.

**Night Side:** The evening shift where crews work stories for the eleven o'clock news. People working on the early shows are "day siders".

**Nuts and Bolts:** Frequently with large stories to which several crews are assigned, one team gets the "nuts and bolts" angle. This is usually a show and tell package that lays out the stories, facts and timeline.

**Package:** The minute and half audio tracked treatment of a story. Also, called a "pack".

**Perp Walk:** It's the picture and sound of the perpetrator being escorted by cops to and from the court house, cop cars, jail basement etc.

**PIO:** Public information officer. The cop or fireman or political group spokesperson. Whoever disseminates information directly to the media from whatever organization is concerned.

**Presser:** Press conference

**Reader:** A story the news anchor reads without any accompanying video.

**Reel:** A quaint throwback to the days when TV news was shot on film. Your reel is a reporter or photographer's best stories collected these days on DVD. For reporter's it includes a good live shot, perhaps some anchoring.

**RF:** The initials stand for radio frequency, which is the condition of hearing an AM radio signal interfering with your audio.

**Rundown:** A producer's list of stories in the order they are to run in the show. The list includes which anchor will read the story or which reporter is presenting it, the total running time of the story and exactly to the second how far each story is in that show.

**Shell:** A reporter's written outline of a story. You may prepare a shell before the story is quite done to speed up the final writing process.

**Siamese Cable:** The twin coaxial and audio cable that runs from the camera to microwave and satellite trucks.

**Slop:** Video at the end of any story, not expected to air, but added in case the story runs long.

**Slot:** The exact spot in a news show where your story will air. It is imperative that you make your slot every single day.

**Slug:** Story title in a producer's rundown.

**S. O. T.:** Acronym for sound on tape. A sound bite.

**Stand Up:** The ten second interlude in a package where the reporter faces the camera and hopefully says something that can't be better said with video or an interview. Often, putting the breaks on an otherwise good story, well done stand ups can pace a story with a few edits during it. Also, it can lead up to or from a picture or sound in an informative way. Good stand ups may have some element of surprise.

**Sticks:** Tripod

**Stripping and Flipping:** A scheme by large media corporations to make a quick profit for a few already wealthy individuals. The new station owner comes in and fires a bunch of station employees in an effort to reduce payroll cost. With the reduced costs usually comes an even greater profit margin. This makes the stripped down station even more attractive financially. So the original owners sell quickly to another large media corporation for a sum often substantially larger than they paid just months before. It's not unusual for the new owners of stations that have been stripped and flipped to swear they are not in the business of stripping and flipping.

**Supers:** Graphics, usually meaning the ones that identify people and locations in stories, running in the lower part of the screen. Short for super imposition.

**Track:** The reporter's pre-recorded sound that's inserted into stories.

**V. J.:** Abbreviation for video journalist or video jockey. Also, called a one man band.

**V. O.:** Abbreviation for voice-over. Voice-overs are the script an anchor or reporter reads while video rolls of the story.

**Vo-Sot:** Voice over-sound on tape abbreviation. The type of story where the anchor or reporter reads live the script while the video plays out. The "sot" is the sound bite that usually follows and is frequently trailed by more v. o.

**Whip:** Popular now with expanded shows and news holes. A whip is just a glorified stand-up but thirty to forty-five seconds long. The reporter tells the bones of the longer package "coming up at five" while walking through the scene of the story.

# Resources

BILL GOETZ IS OUR FRIEND AND FORMER COLLEAGUE. TIM AND I BOTH worked with him during our tenure at KEZI, the ABC affiliate in Eugene, Oregon. Bill was the Chief Photographer there and approached his work with real contemplation, insisting on high standards while helping the rest of us improve our game. His teaching nudges were gentle, but regular and persuasive. Bill's persona didn't necessarily fit the stereotypical image of a chief photographer: Tim's first memory of Bill at KEZI was of a bearded man running through the newsroom on deadline, his Birkenstocks flapping on the floor. But Bill knows when to put his boots on— he is a serious journalist who offers a wealth of information.

At KEZI, Bill routinely went to his mail slot at work, unwrapped and produced new books from Amazon. The titles always had one subject: TV news. Journalism, photojournalism, electronic news gathering or something related. But he wasn't just building a library. Bill reads every book. He knows the subject as well as any professor adding a title to their syllabus. And Bill's list has added weight to it. He applies his readings to his daily work of shooting stories for the local TV news.

Goetz graduated from Whitman College in Washington State and received a Master's Degree in Film from San Francisco State University. He has continued his education at the various workshops and seminars including many offered by the National Press Photographers Association (NPPA) of which he has maintained a decades-long membership. He is currently a staff photographer for KVAL-TV, Eugene's CBS affiliate.

*In 2002, he wrote a three-part article for the NPPA's monthly journal, News Photographer. Bill explored the challenges of working many years in the profession and provided insights into how TV news photographers can choose between making their careers long, hard and depressing or strange, fulfilling and wonderful. We've provided a link.*

*What follows are Bill's recommendations and reviews about organizations and books. Finally, a few choice words about longevity and success, both of which describe Bill's career. We hope you like it as much as we did.*

## Organizations & Workshops

**The National Press Photographers Association**, often referred to as "the NPPA", was founded in 1946 and based in Durham, North Carolina. In its early years, the organization's membership was made up mostly of still, magazine and newspaper photographers. The last forty years have seen steady growth in participation and membership by television news photographers, reporters and, most recently, solo video journalists. The NPPA holds seminars, workshops and competitions to promote the personal, professional and ethical growth of those who dedicate themselves to the highest standards of photojournalism. The NPPA NewsVideo Workshop, held annually at the University of Oklahoma, is widely considered the single best learning experience for those ready to improve upon their skills and abilities. The faculty is comprised of the most highly talented (and awarded) network and local TV photographers and reporters in the business. For more information, see www.nppa.org.

**The Poynter Institute** is a school and a resource for journalism in St. Petersburg, Florida. Education in all aspects of print, still and video journalism as well as management skills for media leaders are offered year around. Training takes place both on campus and via interactive webinars. New course offerings are always being introduced reflecting changes in the profession and Poynter's commitment to be on the cutting edge of teaching and inspiring journalists.

Among the Institute's most popular offerings is "TV Power Reporting." For additional information about this and all course offerings, see www.poynter.org.

## Websites

**B-roll.net Television Photography** (www.b-roll.net). Tips, tricks, news, videos, commentary, product reviews, job listings and blogs can be found in abundance at this site run by Kevin Johnson. B-roll.net's Forum reflects the daily triumphs and frustrations of working in TV News. There is also an educational resource section that offers video critiques and welcomes questions from those just starting out.

**NewsLab** (www.newslab.org). NewsLab is a non-profit online resource to help broadcast journalists build skills and broaden their thinking while maintaining fairness, accuracy and integrity. Just a few mouse clicks will provide access to a wealth of storytelling strategies, tip sheets, research, news and thoughtful analysis about tools, technology and trends in the profession.

**Poynter** (www.poynter.org). In addition to presenting information about classes, seminars and webinars, Poynter provides a useful "How To's" section. There are articles on newsgathering and storytelling strategies as well as news about the media and blogs by Poynter faculty and other media leaders.

## Books

Here is a list of relevant books that may serve as a helpful guide for those who want to know more about a career in local broadcast journalism or just starting their first job as a reporter and/or photographer. It is by no means comprehensive and recent books are not necessarily given preference. Most can be found reasonably priced at amazon.com. Read a book that you found helpful? Share your recommendation at *feedingthebeast.net*.

**Advancing the Story: Broadcast Journalism In A Multimedia World** by Debora Wenger and Deborah Potter (CQ Press College, 2011). Declining viewership and profits have had a profound effect on local television news. The popularity of the Internet as the preferred choice for news and information and the growth of social media have profoundly and irrevocably changed the media landscape for local TV News and the strategies of newsgathering and distribution. This is a well-written text that explains how to effectively use photography, video, print and audio for the Internet.

**ENG: Television News and the New Technology** by Richard Yoakum & Charles Cremer (Second Edition; Random House, 1989). Twenty-plus years ago, the cutting- edge tools of the trade – video cameras and editing, microwave and satellite technology – combined with expanded news programming and the demands of the 24/7 news cycle had a profound impact on how news was gathered and reported. The authors of this text explain how TV journalists can maintain high standards in the field, while avoiding the pitfalls of technology becoming more important than the message.

**The Five C's of Cinematography: Motion Picture Filming Techniques Simplified** by Joseph Mascelli (Silman-James Press, 1998). This was one of the key textbooks I read when I was in film school. It is by far the oldest book listed here (first published in 1965), but still in print because it is so relevant. The Five Cs are camera angles, cutting, composition, close-ups and continuity. They are the grammar of visual storytelling starting back in the era of black-and-white film through videotape to today's digital imagery

**It Takes More Than Good Looks** by Wayne Freedman (Bonus Books, 2003). Currently based at KGO-TV in San Francisco, Wayne Freeman has been telling stories for more than 30 years. Highly regarded as "probably the premier local TV news feature reporter in the country," he has the knack of applying feature techniques to everyday news assignments. There are useful real-world skills and storytelling techniques offered by the author that even small-market novices can use to improve the quality of their work. The book is out of print, but Freedman says he is working on a second edition and updating sections "to reflect the new realities." I am hoping that a DVD of the stories he discusses will be included.

**Make It Memorable: Writing and Packaging TV News with Style** by Bob Dotson (Bonus Books, 2003). For almost 40 years now, Bob Dotson has maintained his unique status as one of the most respected storytellers in the business. He began his career reporting for local stations in the Midwest and later worked for NBC News where his reports have appeared on the *Today Show* and *NBC Nightly News* for more than three decades. He is a favorite with photographers he has worked with and with those he has addressed in workshops and seminars for his view that the photographer is the reporters' best friend. Dotson's book is based on a "story checklist" that has been a part of his lectures for years. There is also a companion videotape of all the stories discussed.

**Roll! Shooting TV News: Views From Behind The Lens** by Rich Underwood (Focal Press, 2007). Author Rich Underwood worked as a staff photographer for KUSA-TV in Denver, a station acclaimed for setting and maintaining a high standard for TV news photography. His book is the ultimate insider's view into the experience, wisdom, creativity and expertise of 19 men and women who make their living at TV News from local to network to broadband. All aspects of news coverage are explored, from breaking news to going live, from shooting from helicopters to using hidden cameras and from one person bands to documentary production. But there is more including practical know-how on lighting, lenses, microphones and cameras plus advice and insight into living the commitment to visual storytelling

**Sequences: Strategies for Shooting News In The Real World** by John Hewitt (Mayfield Publishing Company, 1992). The passage of time hasn't diminished some of the valuable information this "integrated text/videotape package" has to offer. It would be easy to dismiss this work by a San Francisco State University professor as a view from the Ivory Tower. But Hewitt recognized that illustrations were inadequate to the task of illustrating the "complex image stream of a news package with multiple audio layers, dissolves, flash frames" and the impact of images shot and edited in sequences. So an accompanying VHS tape of 54 examples was produced. Once he covers the fundamentals, Hewitt moves on to examine real-world "situational strategies. Used copies of this text cannot always be found with the VHS tape. But even without it, the book is still well worth acquiring.

**Television Field Production And Reporting** by Fred Shook, John Larson & John DeTarsio (Fifth Edition; Allyn & Bacon, 2008). I have not read the current edition, but read the first when it published in 1989. At that time, Shook was beginning a long tenure as faculty member at the NPPA's annual News Video Workshop. Much of the knowledge shared in the Workshop was adapted for this textbook and quite effectively. It is still a relevant resource for beginners and packed with tips that can help professionals "brush up" on their basic skills. While the book is quite expensive, the combined knowledge, experience and expertise it has to offer is worth consideration.

**Working in T.V. News: The Insider's Guide** by Carl Filoreto with Lynn Setzer (Mustang Publishing, 1992). When this book was published, Filoreto was a photographer and Setzer a reporter/ anchor for KMGH-TV in Denver, one of the most competitive local news markets in the country. No updated editions were published and much of the information the authors have to share about the workings of TV News has become somewhat dated. However, much like the book you are holding, Filoreto and Setzer still make pertinent observations about the grind and culture of life in the profession.

K NOWLEDGE, CONSTRUCTIVE FEEDBACK, PRACTICE AND EXPERIENCE ALL help when it comes to being successful in TV News. Some say that learning to make and maintain contacts will help you to move ahead professionally. Reporters have told me that reading — fiction as well as non-fiction — helps them to hone their writing skills. Photographers have said that they have picked up visual story-telling techniques from watching feature films, documentaries and the news stories posted on the websites of TV stations with talented photo staffs, such as KUSA, KARE, WBFF, KING and others.

To all this excellent advice, I would add this: learn how to step back from the grind from time to time and smell the roses. In their book, The Tao of Photography: Seeing Beyond Seeing, authors Philippe Gross and S.I. Shapiro write about achieving "understanding." They write that those photographers who emphasize technical knowledge rely upon "Little Understanding." Those who emphasize informal learning appear to have achieved the perspective of unconstricted awareness or "Greater Understanding." This form of understanding is less about techniques and emphasizes more the ability to feel or see the world with greater consciousness. Ideally, the best photographers have developed the ability to harmonize Little and Great Understanding.

So what does this mean for television news journalists? After all, we are not in the strict sense artists and bound to bend before the truth as we inform viewers of events in our communities. The idea, I think, is to pursue life enhancement, i.e. personal development and understanding. Lynn French, a talented solo journalist for KPNX-TV, makes two practical suggestions in an essay she wrote for b-roll.net a few years ago. She describes subscribing to a magazine that is not TV related and discovers the reading experience is good food for the brain. She also took up an offer for free tickets to an event she would otherwise never attend (as long as it is within her station's policy). She writes, "I have to remind myself these events are very important to someone, they have invested a lot of time and energy in it and it gives a glimpse into a section of society we might not see otherwise. As storytellers, the more we experience other people's lives, the better we can bring them to our viewers." Lynn's on a roll here. Here's one last obvious, but profound observation she has to make. "It is too easy to get immersed in our little news world," she writes. "There is a lot more to life than who was number one in the key demos in early prime fringe during the November book."

Learning is not an end but a lifelong journey. The same applies to continuously embracing a life-enhancing strategy to find out who you are and what you stand for. If you can maintain the balance between the "Little" and "Great" Understanding, a career in TV News does not necessarily have to be a boring grind, but instead a fascinating front-row seat to the ever-changing wonders of the human experience.

**Bill Goetz**
AUGUST 2011

# <u>Dear Students and Colleagues:</u>

I F YOU HAVE MADE IT TO THIS PAGE, WE THANK YOU FOR YOUR ATTENTION, and hope you found our "in the trenches" perspective interesting, helpful, and perhaps amusing! We value your feedback, and ask that you share your thoughts with us about anything you read. Some of these pages have been fairly critical of our profession. We expect a little blow back and are prepared to meet it with an even pulse. But let's talk about it at our website, feedingthebeast.net and keep the conversation going. Feel free to discuss amongst yourselves at the forums provided there. Heartfelt outpourings will be welcomed, as will scathing repudiations or googlemap directions to your favorite fishing hole. Nothing personal, please. Stalkers and kooks must purchase the book before making any threats.

We wish you the best!

Monty and Tim

CPSIA information can be obtained at www.ICGtesting.com
Printed in the USA
LVOW12s2119280414

383562LV00031B/1871/P